CALCULUS FOR PHYSICS

CALCULUS FOR PHYSICS

Richard Dalven
Department of Physics
University of California, Berkeley

McGraw-Hill Book Company

New York St. Louis San Francisco Auckland Bogotá Hamburg
Johannesburg London Madrid Mexico Montreal New Delhi
Panama Paris São Paulo Singapore Sydney Tokyo Toronto

This book was set in Times Roman by Science Typographers, Inc.
The editor was Stephen Zlotnick.
The production supervisor was Diane Renda.
The cover was designed by Fern Logan.
Project supervision was done by The Total Book.
R. R. Donnelley & Sons Company was printer and binder.

CALCULUS FOR PHYSICS

Copyright © 1984 by McGraw-Hill, Inc. All rights reserved.
Printed in the United States of America. Except as permitted under the
United States Copyright Act of 1976, no part of this publication may be
reproduced or distributed in any form or by any means, or stored in a data
base or retrieval system, without the prior written permission of the
publisher.

1 2 3 4 5 6 7 8 9 0 DOCDOC 8 9 8 7 6 5 4

ISBN 0-07-015209-8

Library of Congress Cataloging in Publication Data

Dalven, Richard.
  Calculus for physics.

  Includes index.
  1. Mathematical physics. 2. Calculus. I. Title.
QC20.D25 1984   530.1′55   83-25547
ISBN 0-07-015209-8

This one is for GAIL

CONTENTS

To the Reader ix

Chapter 1 Variables, Functions, and Graphs 1
Introduction 1
Variables and Functions 1
Functional Notation 4
Functions of Several Variables 5
Value of a Function at a Point 6
The Graph of a Function 8
Graphs of Trigonometric Functions.
   Radian Measure 12
Path of a Moving Particle 15

Chapter 2 Derivatives and Differentials 18
Introduction 18
Review of the Definition of the Derivative 18
Calculating Derivatives—A Review 23
The Chain Rule. The Second Derivative 26
Rate of Change 31
Connection between the Derivative and Rate
   of Change 34
Meaning of Instantaneous Rate of Change.
   Functions of Time 38
The Second Derivative and Acceleration 45
Differentials 47
Physical Applications of Differentials 52
The Geometric Interpretation of the Derivative and
   Its Physical Applications 58
Maxima and Minima 66

Chapter 3 Sums and Integrals 71
  Introduction 71
  Review of Integrals as Antiderivatives 71
  Constants of Integration and Initial Conditions 78
  Summation Notation 84
  Review of the Definition of the Definite Integral 85
  Evaluation of Definite Integrals 87
  Geometric Interpretation of the Definite Integral 89
  Interpretation of the Definite Integral as a "Sum of Infinitesimal Elements" 94
  Physical Applications of the Definite Integral 100
  Average Value of a Function 117

Appendix Review of Some Trigonometric Relations 119

Solutions to Exercises 122

Index 141

TO THE READER

The aim of this little book is to "bridge the gap" between the calculus you've learned in your mathematics classes and the calculus used in your physics courses. It has been my experience, based on several years of teaching physics, that many students who are reasonably familiar with the techniques of calculus are not familiar with the meanings of the derivative, differential, and integral when applied to physics. This book is an attempt to help such students and is an outgrowth of notes I distributed in my physics courses.

The book concentrates on explaining the meanings and uses of the key concepts of calculus as applied to elementary physics. However, its aim is not to teach physics per se, and the physics used is kept as simple as possible. The emphasis is on the derivative as a rate of change, the use of differentials as small quantities, and the integral as a sum, all in the context of physics. The book assumes you have taken, or are taking, a course in calculus, so it reviews the definitions and techniques of differentiation and integration, but does not attempt to teach them from the beginning. It is also assumed that you are familiar with elementary algebra and trigonometry, but a brief review of the latter is given in an appendix.

This book is essentially designed for self-study by a student who is beginning to learn physics. I would suggest that you work through the material fairly slowly, using your calculus book to refresh your memory, if necessary, on mathematical points. Most sections of the text conclude with a few exercises. These are designed to reinforce the concepts just presented and to give you practice in using them. The exercises are not meant to be a challenge and are both straightforward and moderate in number so you may realistically do them all. I suggest that you try the exercises as you work through the book. Detailed solutions (not just answers) to the exercises are given in the back of the book and should be consulted after you've given the problems a try.

I've made a real effort to explain the concepts clearly. In fact, you may sometimes think that I'm overexplaining. However, repetition is a useful tool in teaching, and I'd rather say too much about an important topic than say too little. In the same vein, I've tried to write in an informal tone, just as if I were lecturing to a small class. I've also kept this book short by concentrating on material I believe to be really important for physics. Calculus books today seem to run upwards of 1000 pages, possibly making them difficult to use as a reference or for self-study. I hope this little book will help you in your study of physics by making these important ideas more accessible to you.

The book has profited from the valuable comments of Ivanna Juricic, who also read the proofs with a meticulous eye, R. B. Hallock, T. D. MacIver, S. E. Rosser, and S. J. Shepherd, but the responsibility for errors is mine alone. It is again a pleasure to thank John Clarke for his generous hospitality at the Lawrence Berkeley Laboratory. The manuscript was typed with exceptional skill by Claudia Madison, to whom I extend sincere thanks for her help.

Richard Dalven

CHAPTER
ONE
VARIABLES, FUNCTIONS, AND GRAPHS

INTRODUCTION

The aim of this chapter is to introduce much of the terminology we will use in the later chapters, and to review some of the basic concepts you have learned in your calculus course. These are variables, functions, and graphs. The point of view, however, will be that of the physicist, not the mathematician. The concepts we will discuss here are things we will use frequently as we progress.

VARIABLES AND FUNCTIONS

A *variable* is a quantity which may take on different values in the course of the discussion of some question. An example might be the radius r of a circle during a discussion of geometry. The idea of a variable should be contrasted with that of a *constant*, which is a quantity having a fixed value. Examples of constants are the numbers 6, 21, π, etc. The variable (or variables) under consideration in some situation will be denoted by appropriate and convenient symbols; an example is the symbol r for the radius of a circle.

Suppose x and y are both variables. A *function* is a rule connecting the two variables x and y such that, if the value of one variable (say x) is given, the value of the other variable is determined. For example, suppose

$$y = x^2 \qquad (1.1)$$

Eq. (1.1) tells us that the value of the variable y is equal to the square of the value of the variable x. Eq. (1.1) therefore tells us that y is a function of x because, if we know the value of the variable x, the value of the variable y is determined. For example, if $x = 2$, $y = 4$, we say that Eq. (1.1) gives the variable y as a function of the variable x, or, more simply, Eq. (1.1) gives y as a function of x. In Eq. (1.1), assigning a value to x determines the value of y. We call x the *independent variable* in the function $y = x^2$ given in Eq. (1.1). The variable y is called the *dependent variable*, since the value of y depends on the value of x. In discussing Eq. (1.1), we say that y is a function of x, or that there exists a *functional relationship* between the variables y and x.

The function $y = x^2$ in Eq. (1.1) is such that only a single value of the dependent variable y corresponds to each value of the independent variable x. Such a function is called *single-valued*. Functions for which there are more than one value of the dependent variable for each value of the independent variable are called *many-valued* functions. An example of a many-valued function is $y = \pm \sqrt{x}$, in which there are two values of y for each value of x. When we indicate a square root, as in $\sqrt{x}$, or $(1 - x)^{1/2}$, we mean the positive square root; the negative square root would be indicated explicitly, as $-\sqrt{x}$, or $-(1 - x)^{1/2}$. Most of the functions we will encounter will be single-valued.

Given the existence of a functional relationship between the variables y and x, then the set of values which the independent variable x may take on is called the domain of the function. The set of values which the dependent variable y may take on is called the range of the function.

Consider a second example. The familiar relation between the area A of a circle and its radius r is given by Eq. (1.2). Eq. (1.2),

$$A = \pi r^2 \qquad (1.2)$$

expresses the area A as a function of the radius r; π is a constant. From Eq. (1.2), if the value of the independent variable r is specified, then the value of the dependent variable A is determined according to the function (1.2) which gives A as a function of r.

In physics, the variables with which we deal are almost always quantities with a physical meaning and are things that can be measured. For example, the variables A and r in Eq. (1.2) are the area and radius of a circle, both of which are quantities with a physical meaning and which can be measured if we wish. We may contrast the case of Eq. (1.2) with that of Eq. (1.1), in which the variables x and y are mathematical symbols, whose physical meanings (if any) are not specified. In dealing with physical problems, it is helpful to keep in mind the meanings of the symbols with which we deal. In physics, we will constantly be working with functions which give a dependent variable of physical interest in terms of an independent variable (or variables) which will also be physically interesting and measurable quantities.

As a final example of a function, recall the familiar result from elementary physics that "distance equals rate times time" for a body moving with constant rate or speed. If the symbol s is used for distance, v for speed or rate, and t for time, our familiar result is expressed by

$$s = vt \qquad (1.3)$$

Eq. (1.3) gives the distance s (the dependent variable) as a function of the time t (the independent variable) in the case in which the speed v is constant, so v is not a variable in this situation. Eq. (1.3) introduces us to a most important independent variable in physics—the time. Much of physics is concerned with how different quantities vary with time, so physics is often concerned with equations, like Eq. (1.3), giving some quantity *as a function of time*.

Exercises

1.1 Consider the variables w and u connected by the function

$$w = 7u^2 + 6u + 3$$

Which is the independent variable? Which is the dependent variable?

1.2 Eq. (1.1) above gives y as a function of x. Use Eq. (1.1) to obtain an equation giving x as a function of y. In the functional relation you obtained, identify the dependent and independent variables.

1.3 A familiar geometric relation is that between the circumference C and the radius r of a circle, which says that the circumference is the constant 2 times the constant π times the radius of the circle. Write the equation giving C as a function of r. In the functional relation between C and r, which is the dependent and which is the independent variable?

FUNCTIONAL NOTATION

We now discuss a few points concerning the notation used to express functions and functional relationships between variables.

The existence of a general functional relationship between two variables x and y may be indicated by writing

$$y = f(x) \qquad (1.4)$$

an equation which tells us that the dependent variable y is some function f of the independent variable x, but we are not told what the specific function is. Eq. (1.4) does tell us, however, that y is a function of x, so y depends on x. If the specific function f is known, then that information may also be given. For example, in the example in Eq. (1.1) in which $y = x^2$, the specific function f is given, so we may write

$$y = f(x) = x^2 \qquad (1.5)$$

Eq. (1.5) says that the dependent variable y is a function $f(x)$ of the independent variable x, and that the specific function $f(x)$ is x^2.

A situation often encountered in physics is the following. Suppose y is some function f of x, so

$$y = f(x) \qquad (1.6)$$

and the variable x is itself a function g of another variable t, so

$$x = g(t) \qquad (1.7)$$

Eq. (1.6) says y is a function $f(x)$ of the variable x; Eq. (1.7) says x is a function $g(t)$ of the variable t. One can combine Eqs. (1.6) and (1.7) by writing

$$y = f[g(t)] \qquad (1.8)$$

Eq. (1.8) says that the variable y is a function f of the function $g(t)$ of the variable t, so the dependent variable y is ultimately a function of the independent variable t. One also describes the situation in Eq. (1.8) by saying that y is a function f of the function g of t.

As an example, suppose we have the relations

$$y = f(\theta) = \sin \theta \qquad (1.9)$$

$$\theta = g(t) = \omega t \qquad (1.10)$$

where, in Eq. (1.10), ω is a constant. Eq. (1.9) says that the variable y is a function (the sine) of the variable θ, while θ is a function of the variable t. We may combine Eqs. (1.9) and (1.10), using Eq. (1.8), to

give
$$y = \sin \omega t \qquad (1.11)$$
showing that y is a function of t.

Finally, one sometimes sees notation like the following. Suppose y is a function of x; one may write this functional relationship as
$$y = y(x) \qquad (1.12)$$
simply to conserve symbols (which, surprisingly, are sometimes in short supply). Eq. (1.12) says that y is some (unspecified) function of x, so Eq. (1.12) conveys the same information as Eq. (1.6) but uses fewer symbols to do so. In physics, one frequently sees the relations like
$$x = x(t) \qquad (1.13)$$
$$y = y(t) \qquad (1.14)$$
saying that x is a function of t and y is a (different) function of t, so, in Eqs. (1.13) and (1.14), t is the independent variable in both equations.

FUNCTIONS OF SEVERAL VARIABLES

In the preceding sections, we discussed a function
$$y = f(x) \qquad (1.15)$$
in which y depends on the single variable, x. The function $f(x)$ in Eq. (1.15) is a function of one independent variable. We may also consider functions of more than one variable, such as
$$w = g(x, y) \qquad (1.16)$$
Eq. (1.16) says that the dependent variable w is a function of the two independent variables x and y; if values of x and y are specified, then the value of w is determined. Note that the two independent variables x and y are *independent of each other*, so x and y are separate independent variables.

An example of a function of two variables of the type given in Eq. (1.16) is
$$w = g(x, y) = x^2 + y^2 \qquad (1.17)$$
A second example is the expression
$$V = \pi r^2 h \qquad (1.18)$$
for the volume V of a right circular cylinder of radius r and height h.

In Eq. (1.18), V is a function of r and h, both of which are independent variables, so the volume V is a function $V(r, h)$ of r and h. Another example is the function

$$y = y(x, t) = A \sin(kx - \omega t) \tag{1.19}$$

where A, k, and ω are constants. The function in Eq. (1.19) gives y as a sinusoidal function of the two independent variables x and t.

While we will, in this book, usually restrict ourselves to dealing with functions of one variable, we will, on occasion, introduce functions of more than one variable.

VALUE OF A FUNCTION AT A POINT

Generally, the independent variable x in a function

$$y = f(x) \tag{1.20}$$

will take on a set of values called the domain of the function. What this set of values is will be determined by the particular function, the physical situation being discussed, etc. We will often wish to consider the value of the dependent variable y for some *particular* values of x. For example, if

$$y = f(x) = x^2 \tag{1.21}$$

then $y = 4$ when $x = 2$. We say the function $y = f(x) = x^2$ has the value 4 when $x = 2$, or, equivalently, that the function $y = 4$ at the point $x = 2$. (The use of the term *point* for a particular value of x refers to the point on the x axis, such as $x = 2$, corresponding to the value of x. Thus we refer to the value of a function at a point.)

If y is a function $f(x)$ of x, as in Eq. (1.20), then there is a common notation used to indicate the value of $f(x)$ for some particular value of x. It is usual to denote particular values of a variable by putting a subscript on the variable. Thus

$$x = x_1 \tag{1.22}$$

is an equation saying that the variable x has the particular value x_1. In the example above, we consider the case in which x has the value 2, so we were considering

$$x = x_1 = 2 \tag{1.23}$$

meaning that the variable x has the particular value $x_1 = 2$. If, at the same time, we wished to consider a different particular value of x, we

VARIABLES, FUNCTIONS, AND GRAPHS   7

might call it x_2. For example, we might consider
$$x = x_2 = 5 \tag{1.24}$$
as a second particular value of x.

If we are considering a function
$$y = f(x) \tag{1.25}$$
and if the independent variable x has the value x_1 so
$$x = x_1 \tag{1.26}$$
then we indicate the value of the function $f(x)$ when x has the value x_1 by the notation
$$f(x_1) \tag{1.27}$$
Expression (1.27) stands for the value of the function $f(x)$ when $x = x_1$, or, saying it in another way, the value of the function $f(x)$ at the point $x = x_1$. As an example, let's return to the function
$$y = f(x) = x^2 \tag{1.28}$$
and find the value of the function (1.28) when x has the value 2, i.e., when
$$x = x_1 = 2 \tag{1.29}$$
Using the notation described above, we have
$$f(x_1) = (x_1)^2 = (2)^2 = 4 \tag{1.30}$$
Since $x_1 = 2$, we can (and will often) also write
$$f(2) \tag{1.31}$$
for the value of the function $f(x)$ when $x = 2$. Similarly, when $x = 5$, $f(5)$ is the value of the function $f(x)$ when $x = 5$.

To summarize, if y is a function $f(x)$ of x, so $y = f(x)$, then $f(x_1)$ is the value of the dependent variable y, and of the function f, when the independent variable x has the value x_1.

These ideas may be extended to a function of several variables. Suppose
$$w = f(x, y) \tag{1.32}$$
is a function of the two variables x and y. Then
$$f(x_1, y_1)$$
is the value of the function f when x has the value x_1 (i.e., $x = x_1$) and y has the value y_1 (i.e., $y = y_1$). For example, suppose
$$w = f(x, y) = x^2 + y^2 \tag{1.33}$$

What is the value of $f(0, 2)$, which is the value of the function f when $x = 0$ and $y = 2$? From Eq. (1.33),

$$f(0, 2) = (0)^2 + (2)^2 = 4 \qquad (1.34)$$

Note also that we may sometimes wish to consider a function like $f(x, y)$ for a particular value of one independent variable but for *any* value of the other independent variable. As an example consider the function f in Eq. (1.33) when $x = 0$; then we have

$$f(0, y) = y^2 \qquad (1.35)$$

as the value of $f(x, y)$ when $x = 0$. In this case the "value" of $f(0, y)$ is itself a function (in this case the function y^2) and not just a number.

Exercises

1.4 Given the function
$$y = f(x) = 3x^2 + 2$$
Find (a) $f(2)$; (b) $f(0)$; (c) $f(-1)$.

1.5 Given the function
$$y(x, t) = A \sin(kx - \omega t)$$
where A, k, and ω are constants. Find expressions for: (a) $y(0, 0)$; (b) $y(0, t)$; (c) $y(x, 0)$

1.6 Given the function $y = f(x) = (1 - x^2)^{1/2}$. Find $f(x - a)$, where a is a constant. Note that $f(x - a)$ is obtained by replacing the independent variable x in $f(x)$ by the new variable $(x - a)$.

THE GRAPH OF A FUNCTION

When we are considering a function, it is usual in physics to display the functional relationship between the dependent and independent variables by means of a *graph* of the function. Suppose we are considering a function

$$y = f(x) \qquad (1.36)$$

We can assign a series of values to the independent variable x, and, from the functional relationship in Eq. (1.36), obtain the corresponding values of the dependent variable y. For example, if the specific function under discussion were

$$y = f(x) = x^2 \qquad (1.37)$$

we would obtain the table of values below for integral

x	0	1	2	3	4	5
y	0	1	4	9	16	25

values of x between 0 and 5. However, it is difficult from a table of values to "see" the behavior of the function $f(x)$ as x takes on various values. For this reason it is usual to construct a graph of the function.

The definition of a graph is as follows. The graph of the function $f(x)$ is the set of all points with rectangular coordinates $(x, f(x))$. Here the notation $(x, f(x))$ means the point whose abscissa (x coordinate) has the value x and whose ordinate (y coordinate) has the value $f(x)$. For our example in Eq. (1.37), the graph of the function $y = f(x) = x^2$ is the set of all points with coordinates (x, x^2). Six such points, $(0, 0)$, $(1, 1)$, $(2, 4)$, $(3, 9)$, $(4, 16)$, and $(5, 25)$ are seen in the table above. These six points are, of course, not *all* of the points comprising the graph of the function $y = f(x) = x^2$; there are an infinite number of other points, such as $(2.5, 6.25)$, with the form (x, x^2).

If we plot, in two dimensions, all of the points of the form $(x, f(x))$, we obtain the graph of $f(x)$. For our example, we plot points of the form (x, x^2) and obtain the graph shown in Fig. 1.1. In that figure, we plot $y = f(x) = x^2$ vertically (ordinate) and x horizontally (abscissa) and obtain the curve shown in the figure. The graph is the set of all points whose coordinates (x, y) satisfy the functional

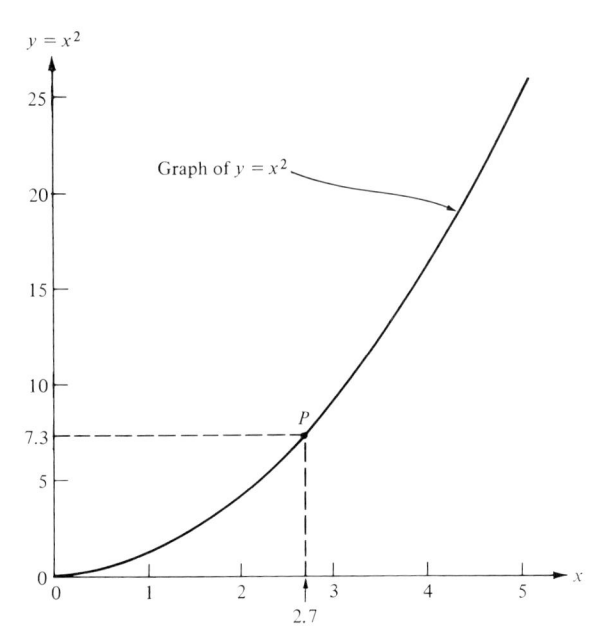

Figure 1.1 Graph of the function $y = f(x) = x^2$ for $0 \le x \le 5$.

relation $y = x^2$ given in Eq. (1.37). Therefore, any point on the graph (or curve, as it is also called) has coordinates (x, y) such that $y = x^2$. The point P, for example, has coordinates (2.7, 7.29). From the figure, we can "see" how the function $y = f(x) = x^2$ varies with x.

In general, then, if we have the graph of the function $y = f(x)$ plotted as a function of x, we may find the value of the function for any value $x = x_1$ of x by reading it off the graph. The point $(x_1, f(x_1))$ will be a point on the graph, so, knowing the value of x_1 determines the value of $f(x_1)$. In Fig. 1.1, in which $f(x) = x^2$, we considered the point $x_1 = 2.7$ on the x axis; the y coordinate of the point P can be read to be $f(x_1) \cong 7.3$, as shown in the curve in the figure. Note that we can read the value of $f(x_1) = f(2.7)$ off the graph in Fig. 1.1 only approximately. From the graph, we read $f(2.7) \cong 7.3$, which may be compared with the exact value $f(2.7) = (2.7)^2 = 7.29$. (It should be pointed out that, in physics, the reading of graphs in this manner is frequently necessary for graphs of experimental data for which the functional relationship is not known. In such cases, the reading of values is necessarily approximate.)

There are a number of functions of one variable whose graphs are frequently encountered in physics. One is the parabola, an example of which is seen in the graph of $y = x^2$ in Fig. 1.1. From analytic geometry, we know that the general quadratic equation

$$y = f(x) = ax^2 + bx + c \qquad (1.38)$$

where a, b, and c are constants, has as its graph a parabola whose axis is parallel to the y axis. In our example above, in Eq. (1.37), $y = x^2$ is the special case of Eq. (1.38) for which $a = 1$ and $b = c = 0$.

A second important function in physics is of the form

$$y = f(x) = mx + b \qquad (1.39)$$

where m and b are constants. Eq. (1.39) shows a function whose graph is a straight line of slope m which passes through the point whose coordinates are $y = b$, $x = 0$. We recall that the slope m of the straight line (1.39) is defined as the tangent of the angle the line makes with the positive direction of the x axis. The point $(0, b)$ is called the y intercept of the line. As an example, consider the function

$$y = f(x) = 2x + 1 \qquad (1.40)$$

whose graph is shown in Fig. 1.2 for values of x between 0 and 3. Comparison of the function in Eq. (1.40) with the general form of the straight line given in Eq. (1.39) shows that the y intercept is at the point (0, 1) so $b = 1$ in Eq. (1.39). In the Fig. 1.2, θ is the angle

VARIABLES, FUNCTIONS, AND GRAPHS 11

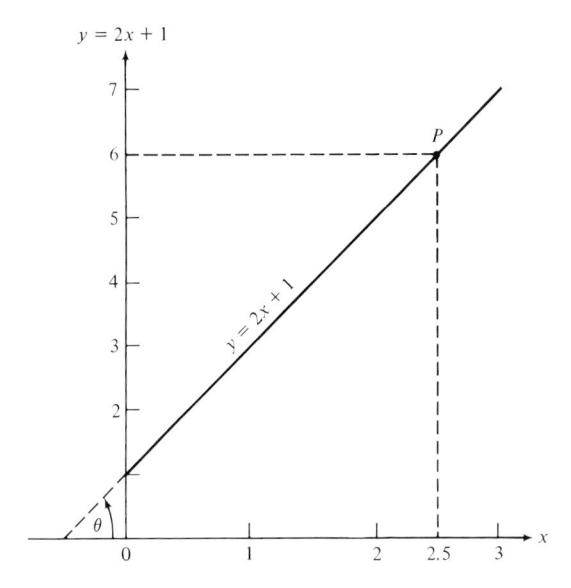

Figure 1.2 Graph of $y = f(x) = 2x + 1$ for $0 \le x \le 3$.

between the straight line and the x axis. Then, from the definition of the slope, we have from Eq. (1.39) that

$$m = \tan \theta = 2 \tag{1.41}$$

leading to the value $\theta = \tan^{-1} 2 = 63.4° = 1.11$ rad (radian measure of angles is discussed below). Any point, such as P in Fig. 1.2, on the graph of the function in Eq. (1.40) has coordinate $(x, (2x + 1))$. For example, if $x = 2.5$, $y = 2x + 1 = 6$, we have point P whose coordinates are $(2.5, 6)$.

Exercises

1.7 Consider the function

$$y = f(x) = x - 2x^2$$

(a) Calculate the value of y for values of x from $x = 0$ to $x = 0.5$ in increments of 0.05; (b) Using graph paper, draw the graph of $f(x)$ as a function of x; (c) What is the name of this curve?; (d) From your graph, determine the value of y when $x = 0.32$; (e) For what values of x does $y = 0$?

1.8 (a) What is the equation of a straight line of slope 2 passing through the origin? (b) What angle does this line make with the x axis?; (c) Make a graph of this function for values of x from 0 to 2.

12 CALCULUS FOR PHYSICS

1.9 In Exercise 6 (above), you were given $y = f(x) = (1 - x^2)^{1/2}$ and found the new function $y = f(x - a) = [1 - (x - a)^2]^{1/2}$. (a) On graph paper, make a careful graph of $f(x - a)$ as a function of x for the value of the constant $a = 0$. Use values of x between $x = 1$ and $x = -1$ (inclusive) at intervals of 0.2; (b) Repeat the graph of $f(x - a)$ for $a = 4$ for values of x between $x = 3$ and $x = 5$ (inclusive), also at intervals of 0.2. Consider only positive values of y in making your tables and graphs.

GRAPHS OF TRIGONOMETRIC FUNCTIONS. RADIAN MEASURE

The graphs of the trigonometric functions $\sin x$ and $\cos x$ are often encountered in physics. In order to discuss these functions, it is necessary to introduce the measurement of angles in *radians*. Fig. 1.3 shows a circle of radius r with two points, A and B, on its circumference; radii are drawn from the center O to points A and B. The distance along the circumference between A and B is denoted by s and is called the *arc length* between A and B; θ is the angle between the radii OA and OB. With this notation, the magnitude of the angle θ, in radians, is given by the equation

$$\theta = \frac{s}{r} \text{ (radians)} \qquad (1.42)$$

From Eq. (1.42), we can see that the angle θ has the value 1 radian when the arc length s subtended by the angle θ is equal to the radius r of the circle. (Note that, from Eq. (1.42), the quantity (s/r) is dimensionless because it is the ratio of two lengths. The radian is thus really a number of geometric significance and is not a "unit" in the

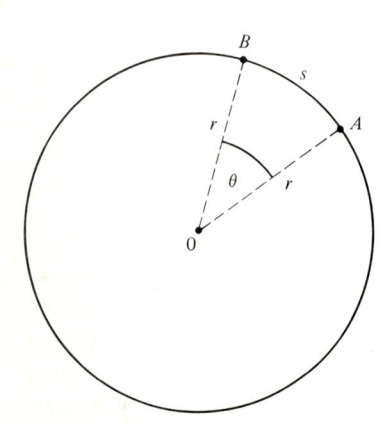

Figure 1.3 Circle used in defining radian measure.

VARIABLES, FUNCTIONS, AND GRAPHS 13

sense in which we use the term in physics.) We recall that the circumference C of a circle is related to its radius r by the relation

$$C = 2\pi r \tag{1.43}$$

so the arc length of the entire circumference of a circle of radius r is equal to $2\pi r$. If we set the arc length s equal to $2\pi r$ in Eq. (1.42), we obtain

$$\theta = \frac{2\pi r}{r} = 2\pi \text{ (radians)} \tag{1.44}$$

Eq. (1.44) says that the number of radians in a complete circle of 360° in 2π rad. Since 360° is equal to 2π radians,

$$1 \text{ rad} = \frac{360°}{2\pi} \cong 57.3° \tag{1.45}$$

so 1 rad is (approximately) equal to 57.3°. In physics, angles are very frequently measured in radians, and some common angles are given below in radians.

$$45° = (\pi/4) \text{ radians}$$
$$90° = (\pi/2) \text{ radians}$$
$$180° = \pi \text{ radians}$$
$$360° = 2\pi \text{ radians} \tag{1.46}$$

As a final point on radian measure, we note that Eq. (1.42) can be rewritten as

$$s = r\theta \tag{1.47}$$

Eq. (1.47) gives the arc length s along a circle of radius r in terms of the angle θ subtended by that arc length. For example, in a circle of radius 1 meter an angle of 0.1 radian would subtend an arc length $s = (1)(0.1) = 0.1$ meters. It is important to keep in mind in using Eqs. (1.47) and (1.42) that the angle θ must be expressed in radians.

We now consider the graph of the important trigonometric function

$$y = f(x) = \sin x \tag{1.48}$$

As with any other graph of a function $f(x)$, every point on the graph of the function in Eq. (1.48) will have a coordinate of the form $(x, f(x))$, so the points comprising the graph of $\sin x$ will have coordinates $(x, \sin x)$, where x is an angle in radians. Fig. 1.4 shows the graph of $y = \sin x$ as a function of x; as is customary, the angle x (in radians) is plotted in multiples of π. Examining the graph of $\sin x$ in Fig. 1.4, we see that $\sin x$ is positive for values of x between $x = 0$ and $x = \pi$ radians, and that $\sin x$ is negative for values of x between π

14 CALCULUS FOR PHYSICS

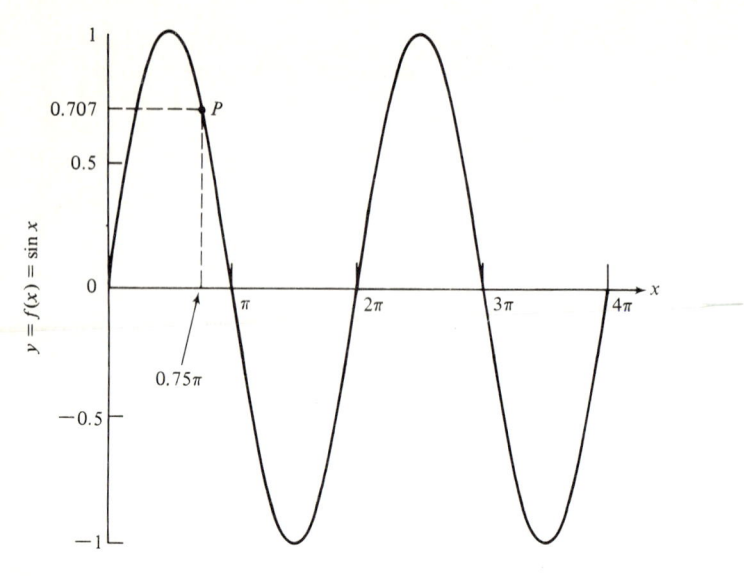

Figure 1.4 Graph of $y = f(x) = \sin x$ for $0 \leq x \leq 4\pi$.

and 2π radians. Each point on the graph has coordinates $(x, \sin x)$; for example, point P has coordinates $((3\pi/4), 0.707)$.

Let us describe the variation of $y = \sin x$ as x increases from 0 to 2π radians. When $x = 0$, $y = 0$; as x increases, y increases and reaches its maximum value of unity (i.e., 1) when $x = (\pi/2)$ radians. As x increases further, y decreases, reaching the value zero when $x = \pi$ radians; y continues to decrease with increasing x until y reaches its minimum value of (-1) when $x = (3\pi/2)$ radians. As x increases beyond $(3\pi/2)$ radians, y increases from (-1), reaching the value zero when $x = 2\pi$ radians. We have just described the variation of $y = \sin x$ as x varies from zero to 2π radians. This variation is often referred to as one *cycle* of the sine function because, as x increases beyond 2π radians, the variation shown in Fig. 1.4 is repeated for values of x between 2π and 4π radians. The variation of $\sin x$ with x is thus repetitive, or *periodic*, with a period of 2π radians. One refers to the set of values of x over which $\sin x$ varies through one cycle as the *period* of the sine function; the period of the sine function is thus 2π radians.

As a last point, we may mention the following useful fact. If θ is a small angle and is expressed in *radians*, then

$$\theta \cong \sin \theta \cong \tan \theta \qquad (1.49)$$

Eq. (1.49) says that, for a small angle θ expressed in radians, the numerical value of θ is approximately equal to the sine of θ, which is approximately equal to the tangent of θ. For example, suppose $\theta = (\pi/100)$ radians, so θ is 1.8°. Then $\theta = 0.03142$ radians, $\sin\theta = 0.03141$, $\tan\theta = 0.03143$, and we can see that the relation in Eq. (1.49) is satisfied to within about one part in 3000, or about 0.03 percent. The smaller the angle θ, the more accurate is relation (1.49), which is usually called the *small angle approximation*. For how large a value of θ is Eq. (1.49) valid? The answer depends on how accurately you wish Eq. (1.49) to be satisfied. For example, if $\theta = (\pi/20)$ radians = 0.1571 radians (about 9°), then $\sin\theta = 0.1564$ and $\tan\theta = 0.1584$. Thus, for this larger angle, the relation in Eq. (1.49) is valid to only about 1 percent. The small angle approximation is often used to deal with the trigonometric functions of small angles.

Exercises

1.10 Calculate the number of degrees in the following angles:
(a) $(\pi/8)$ radians; (b) $(3\pi/4)$ radians; (c) 3π radians; (d) $(31\pi/32)$ radians.

1.11 (a) Make a table giving values of $\cos x$ for values of x from 0 to 4π radians, inclusive. Calculate values at intervals of $(\pi/8)$ radians. (b) Using graph paper, make a graph of $\cos x$ as a function of x for $0 \le x \le 4\pi$ radians. (c) What are the maximum and minimum values of $\cos x$? (d) Is the function $f(x) = \cos x$ periodic with x? Give the reason for your answer; (e) What is the period of the function $\cos x$? (f) How many cycles of the function $\cos x$ are there on the graph in Part (b)? (g) Using your graph, find the value of $\cos(39\pi/16)$ and compare the value you read from the graph with the value from your calculator. (Note to the student: This rather tedious exercise gives you practice in a number of useful skills, including the use of radian measure, making graphs, interpreting graphs, and calculating trigonometric values.)

PATH OF A MOVING PARTICLE

An important type of graph in physics is the path or trajectory of a particle (or any other kind of body) as it moves through space. This path is the set of points in space successively occupied by the particle as it moves with increasing time. Generally, the path of a moving particle is denoted by specifying the equation of the mathematical curve composed of the set of points occupied by the moving particle. For example, suppose that a particle is moving in a circular path, of radius r, in a horizontal plane. Let us define that horizontal plane as the xy plane and let us choose the origin of coordinates at the center of the circular path. Then the path traced out by the particle as it moves is a circle of radius r centered at the origin, so every point on the path satisfies the equation

$$x^2 + y^2 = r^2 \qquad (1.50)$$

This means that every point, of coordinates (x, y), that the particle passes through as it moves will have x and y values which satisfy Eq. (1.50). We recall that Eq. (1.50) is the equation of a circle of radius r, centered at the origin, in the xy plane. When, in physics, we speak of a particle moving in a path given by some particular equation, the idea above is what is meant.

It is usual, however, to find that information on the path of a moving particle is given in a form different from Eq. (1.50). Eq. (1.50) gives the equation of the path of the particle in space. It is more useful in many situations to have information on the position of a moving particle as a function of time. This is generally given by specifying the coordinates, such as the rectangular coordinates (x, y, z) of the particle as functions of time, as

$$x = f(t); \; y = g(t); \; z = h(t) \qquad (1.51)$$

Eq. (1.51) says that the x coordinate of the moving particle is a function $f(t)$ of the time t, etc. With equations of the type in Eq. (1.51), one can calculate the coordinates (x, y, z) of the particle at any value of the time t. Equations of the form in Eq. (1.51) are called *parametric* equations because they give x, y, and z as functions of another variable t, where t is called the parameter.

As an example, let's consider again the particle moving in the xy plane in a horizontal circle of radius r, now adding for convenience the stipulation that the velocity v of the particle is constant. (The velocity v is the tangential velocity of the particle, not its angular velocity.) In analytic geometry it is shown that the parametric equations of the circle in Eq. (1.50) are

$$x = r \cos \theta \qquad (1.52)$$

$$y = r \sin \theta \qquad (1.53)$$

which can be seen to be true by verifying that substitutions of Eqs. (1.52) and (1.53) satisfy Eq. (1.50). In your physics course, you will find out that the parameter θ in Eqs. (1.52) and (1.53) is given by

$$\theta = (vt/r) \qquad (1.54)$$

where v is the particle's velocity, r is the radius of the circular path, and t is the time. Substituting Eq. (1.54) into Eqs. (1.52) and (1.53)

gives us
$$x = r\cos(vt/r) \quad (1.55)$$
$$y = r\sin(vt/r) \quad (1.56)$$
as the parametric equations, of the form in Eq. (1.51), of the circular path of the particle. The important thing about Eqs. (1.55) and (1.56) is that they give us the x and y coordinates of the particle as functions of time. This enables us to calculate the coordinates (x, y) of the position of the particle at any instant of time we like.

For example, suppose the velocity $v = 10$ m/s and the radius $r = 10$ m. Then Eqs. (1.55) and (1.56) become
$$x = 10\cos t \quad (1.57)$$
$$y = 10\sin t \quad (1.58)$$
Let us calculate the coordinates (x, y) of the position of the particle when the time $t = 1$ s. Then
$$x = 10\cos 1 = 10(0.540) = 5.40 \text{ m} \quad (1.59)$$
where, in Eq. (1.59), the angle is in radians, so we are taking the cosine of 1 rad. Similarly,
$$y = 10\sin 1 = 10(0.841) = 8.41 \text{ m} \quad (1.60)$$
so the coordinates of the moving particle at the instant $t = 1$ s are
$$(x = 5.40 \text{ m}, y = 8.41 \text{ m})$$

You will frequently encounter paths of moving particles in physics, and they will often be given in parametric form like Eqs. (1.55) and (1.56). One of the most important examples will be the parametric equations of the two-dimensional parabolic path of the projectile, giving the projectile's coordinates (x, y) as functions of time.

CHAPTER
TWO
DERIVATIVES AND DIFFERENTIALS

INTRODUCTION

The aim of this chapter is to review some topics in differential calculus and to describe some applications to physics. In particular, the idea of the derivative as a rate of change is emphasized because of its central importance in physics. Special attention is given to dealing with functions of time. The notion of the differential, sometimes neglected in calculus courses, is also given emphasis because of its frequent use in elementary physics. Finally, some of the applications of the geometric interpretation of the derivative are considered.

REVIEW OF THE DEFINITION OF THE DERIVATIVE

We begin by *reviewing* the definition of the derivative on the assumption that you have already studied this material in your calculus course. If your notion of a *limit* is vague, this would be a good point at which to refresh your memory by reviewing limits in your calculus text.
    Suppose we have a function $f(x)$ of the independent variable x. We will tacitly assume that the function $f(x)$ is a "well-behaved"

DERIVATIVES AND DIFFERENTIALS 19

function, which we will, rather casually, take to mean that all of the relevant limits exist and that $f(x)$ exhibits no cusps, discontinuities, or other exceptional features which may cause difficulty. Consider the value

$$f(x_1) \qquad (2.1)$$

of the function at some point $x = x_1$ and consider also the value

$$f(x_1 + \Delta x) \qquad (2.2)$$

at a second point $x = (x_1 + \Delta x)$. The quantity Δx is called the *increment* in the variable x and is the amount of change in the variable x when x varies from the value x_1 to the value $(x_1 + \Delta x)$. (Keep in mind that Δx is really a single symbol, read "delta-x," and is *not* the product of Δ and x.)

Next, we form the quotient

$$\frac{f(x_1 + \Delta x) - f(x_1)}{\Delta x} \qquad (2.3)$$

and consider what happens when the increment Δx gets very small. The process of Δx getting very small (as small as we wish) is symbolized by writing

$$\Delta x \to 0 \qquad (2.4)$$

an expression which is read "Δx approaches zero." To define the *derivative* of the function $f(x)$, we examine what happens to the expression in Eq. (2.3) as Δx gets very small. The limit of expression (2.3) as Δx gets very small is written

$$\lim_{\Delta x \to 0} \frac{f(x_1 + \Delta x) - f(x_1)}{\Delta x} \qquad (2.5)$$

and will be assumed to exist in the cases of physical interest which we will consider. The limit given in Eq. (2.5) is defined as the derivative of the function $f(x)$ at the point $x = x_1$ and is written

$$f'(x_1) \qquad (2.6)$$

an expression which is read "f prime at x_1" or "f prime of x_1."

To summarize so far, the derivative $f'(x_1)$ of the function $f(x)$ at the point $x = x_1$ is defined as

$$f'(x_1) = \lim_{\Delta x \to 0} \frac{f(x_1 + \Delta x) - f(x_1)}{\Delta x} \qquad (2.7)$$

again assuming that the limit exists at the point $x = x_1$. For the functions we will consider in our physics examples, we will assume

20 CALCULUS FOR PHYSICS

that the appropriate limit in Eq. (2.7) exists for *all* values of x under consideration. Thus the point x_1 can be *any* point x in the set of values which the independent variable x may take on. We may therefore replace x_1 in Eq. (2.7) by x since x_1 can be any value of x. Doing this, Eq. (2.7) becomes

$$f'(x) = \lim_{\Delta x \to 0} \frac{f(x + \Delta x) - f(x)}{\Delta x} \qquad (2.8)$$

Eq. (2.8) defines the derivative $f'(x)$ of the function $f(x)$.

As an example which will illuminate the definition, let us calculate the derivative of a simple function using the definition (2.8). Suppose the function f is

$$f(x) = 2x^2 \qquad (2.9)$$

Then

$$f(x + \Delta x) = 2(x + \Delta x)^2 \qquad (2.10)$$

is the value of the function f at the point $(x + \Delta x)$. Evaluating the expression in Eq. (2.10) gives us

$$f(x + \Delta x) = 2\left(x^2 + 2x(\Delta x) + (\Delta x)^2\right)$$

$$f(x + \Delta x) = 2x^2 + 4x(\Delta x) + 2(\Delta x)^2 \qquad (2.11)$$

so we obtain next

$$f(x + \Delta x) - f(x) = 2x^2 + 4x(\Delta) + (\Delta x)^2 - 2x^2$$

$$= 4x(\Delta x) + (\Delta x)^2 \qquad (2.12)$$

Dividing expression (2.12) by the quantity Δx gives

$$\frac{f(x + \Delta x) - f(x)}{\Delta x} = \frac{4x(\Delta x) + (\Delta x)^2}{\Delta x} = 4x + (\Delta x) \qquad (2.13)$$

The next step in applying the definition (2.8) of the derivative is to take the limit of the expression (2.13) as $\Delta x \to 0$, so we have

$$\lim_{\Delta x \to 0} \frac{f(x + \Delta x) - f(x)}{\Delta x} = \lim_{\Delta x \to 0} (4x + \Delta x) = 4x \qquad (2.14)$$

From the result in Eq. (2.14), we have

$$f'(x) = 4x \qquad (2.15)$$

as the derivative of the function $f(x) = 2x^2$. (It should be pointed out that the step of taking the limit as $\Delta x \to 0$ is not usually as simple as the one in Eq. (2.14); see your calculus text for details, techniques, and examples.) We note also that, in Eq. (2.15), the derivative $f'(x)$ is itself a function of x.

In summary, the definition of the derivative $f'(x)$ of the function $f(x)$ is given by

$$f'(x) \equiv \lim_{\Delta x \to 0} \frac{f(x + \Delta x) - f(x)}{\Delta x} \qquad (2.8)$$

We will see in later sections how this definition is useful in describing physical (and geometric) situations.

We conclude with a few remarks about the nomenclature and notation for the derivative $f'(x)$. Since we are finding the derivative of a function $f(x)$ of the variable x, $f'(x)$ is often referred to as the derivative of f *with respect to* x and the process of calculating $f'(x)$ is often called differentiation with respect to x. (It may seem overly precise to specify the variable, e.g., x, with respect to which we are calculating the derivative, but this usage focuses attention on the independent variable involved. Furthermore, in dealing with functions of more than one variable, it is essential to specify which variable is involved in the derivative.)

While the notation $f'(x)$ is very common, there are others, some of which are particularly useful in physics. Another notation for the derivative of $f(x)$ is

$$\frac{df}{dx} \qquad (2.16)$$

Formally, we may define the expression (2.16) by the relation

$$\frac{df}{dx} \equiv f'(x) \qquad (2.17)$$

which simply says that the symbol (df/dx) means the derivative $f'(x)$. (Incidentally, the symbol (df/dx), written on a line, is identical to the form in expressions (2.16) and (2.17). Writing it (df/dx) simply saves space in the text.) Similarly, if the dependent variable y is related to the function $f(x)$ by

$$y = f(x) \qquad (2.18)$$

we may write the derivative of the function f as y', so

$$y' \equiv f'(x) \qquad (2.19)$$

Still another notation is often used. When y is a function of x, as in Eq. (2.18), the derivative $f'(x)$ is sometimes written as

$$\frac{dy}{dx} \qquad (2.20)$$

22 CALCULUS FOR PHYSICS

which you may also see written on a line as (dy/dx) to save space. The meaning of the expression (2.20) is defined by the relation

$$\frac{dy}{dx} \equiv f'(x) \qquad (2.21)$$

Eq. (2.21) simply says that, if $y = f(x)$, then the symbol (dy/dx) means the derivative $f'(x)$. The expression (dy/dx) is read "the derivative of y with respect to x."

Keep in mind that (at least for now) the symbols (df/dx) and (dy/dx) are *not* to be considered as quotients. It is especially important to realize that, in calculus, the symbol dy does *not* ever mean a quantity d times a quantity y. The same is true for df; in calculus, it *never* means d times f. Among other things, this means that it is wrong and without meaning to attempt to "cancel" the d's in (dy/dx) or (df/dx). For now, we will consider the symbols (dy/dx) and (df/dx) as single symbols for the derivative $f'(x)$.

As a last point in this section, suppose we know that y is some function of x, so

$$y = f(x) \qquad (2.22)$$

a functional relationship in which y is the dependent and x is the independent variable. If we were to solve Eq. (2.22) for x as a function of y, we would obtain

$$x = g(y) \qquad (2.23)$$

where Eq. (2.23) is the function *inverse* to Eq. (2.22). In Eq. (2.23), x is the dependent variable and y is the independent variable. A useful theorem relates (dy/dx), the derivative of y with respect to x, and (dx/dy), the derivative of x with respect to y, where

$$(dy/dx) \equiv f'(x); \; (dx/dy) \equiv g'(y) \qquad (2.24)$$

in our usual notation. The theorem states as its result that

$$f'(x) = \frac{1}{g'(y)} \qquad (2.25)$$

or, alternatively,

$$\frac{dy}{dx} = \frac{1}{\frac{dx}{dy}} \qquad (2.26)$$

The result in Eq. (2.25) or Eq. (2.26) is often useful in the calculation of derivatives. Note that this result assumes that $g'(y)$ is not equal to zero.

Exercises

2.1 Using the definition in Eq. (2.8), find the derivative $f'(x)$ of the function $f(x) = x^3$. The aim of this exercise is not so much to obtain the derivative itself, but to see how the definition leads to the derivative.

2.2 Using the definition in Eq. (2.8), find the derivative $f'(x)$ of the function $f(x) = (1/x)$, where $x \neq 0$. Again, the aim of the exercise is to illustrate the definition of the derivative.

CALCULATING DERIVATIVES—A REVIEW

In your calculus course, you learned how to calculate the derivatives of various kinds of functions; it is assumed you have seen them before in your calculus course. Some of the derivatives are reviewed in this section. It will be useful to introduce another common notation at this point. One often sees the symbols

$$\frac{d}{dx}[f(x)] = f'(x) \tag{2.27}$$

used for the derivative $f'(x)$. The left-hand side of Eq. (2.27) is used to indicate the *operation or process* of calculating the derivative $f'(x)$ of the function $f(x)$. One would read Eq. (2.27) by saying "the operation of taking the derivative of the function $f(x)$ yields $f'(x)$." As an example of this notation, consider the function $f(x) = 2x^2$ given in Eq. (2.9); in Eq. (2.15), we found the derivative $f'(x) = 4x$. In the notation of Eq. (2.27), we would write

$$\frac{d}{dx}[2x^2] = 4x \tag{2.28}$$

Eq. (2.28) says that the operation or process of calculating the derivative of the function $2x^2$ produces $4x$, where $f'(x) = 4x$ is the derivative of the function $f(x) = 2x^2$. Another example would be

$$\frac{d}{dx}[x^3] = 3x^2 \tag{2.29}$$

Eq. (2.29) says that the derivative of the function x^3 is $3x^2$. This notation will be used in the review of derivatives below. All of the following derivatives follow directly from the definition in Eq. (2.8) and can be obtained (albeit with some difficulty) in the same way as were the examples in Exercises 2.1 and 2.2.

If c is a constant, then the derivative of c is zero. This is expressed in the equation

$$\frac{d}{dx}[c] = 0 \tag{2.30}$$

where Eq. (2.30) states that the derivative of any constant is zero.

24 CALCULUS FOR PHYSICS

Suppose
$$u = u(x)$$
and
$$v = v(x)$$
are two functions of the independent variable x. Then the derivative of the *sum* of the two functions is the sum of the derivatives, so we have

$$\frac{d}{dx}[u + v] = \frac{du}{dx} + \frac{dy}{dx} = u'(x) + v'(x) \qquad (2.31)$$

In Eq. (2.31), we exhibit two different notations, (du/dx) and $u'(x)$, for the derivative of the function $u(x)$ with respect to x, and the same for the derivative of $v(x)$.

If we consider the derivative of a constant c times a function $u = u(x)$, we have that

$$\frac{d}{dx}[cu] = c\frac{du}{dx} = cu'(x) \qquad (2.32)$$

Eq. (2.32) says that the derivative of a constant times a function is equal to the constant times the derivative of the function.

As an example of the use of these results, consider the functions

$$u(x) = 6x^3; \; v(x) = \frac{2}{x}$$

and find the derivative of the function $(6x^3 + (2/x))$. Then

$$\frac{d}{dx}\left[6x^3 + \frac{2}{x}\right] = \frac{d}{dx}[6x^3] + \frac{d}{dx}\left[\frac{2}{x}\right]$$

from Eq. (2.31). From Eq. (2.32), we have

$$\frac{d}{dx}[6x^3] = 6\frac{d}{dx}[x^3]$$
$$\frac{d}{dx}\left[\frac{2}{x}\right] = 2\frac{d}{dx}\left[\frac{1}{x}\right] \qquad (2.33)$$

The derivatives of x^3 and $(1/x)$ were found in Exercises 1 and 2 as $3x^2$ and $(-1/x^2)$, respectively, so the final answer is

$$\frac{d}{dx}\left[6x^3 + \frac{2}{x}\right] = 6(3x^2) + 2\left(\frac{-1}{x^2}\right) = 18x^2 - \frac{2}{x^2} \qquad (2.34)$$

We now review the derivatives of some of the elementary functions commonly encountered in physics.

The derivative of a power n of a variable x is given by

$$\frac{d}{dx}[x^n] = nx^{n-1} \qquad (2.35)$$

An example would be

$$\frac{d}{dx}[x^4] = 4x^3 \tag{2.36}$$

The derivative of the exponential function e^x is

$$\frac{d}{dx}[e^x] = e^x \tag{2.37}$$

The derivatives of two important trigonometric functions are as follows.

$$\frac{d}{dx}[\sin x] = \cos x \tag{2.38}$$

$$\frac{d}{dx}[\cos x] = -\sin x \tag{2.39}$$

Next, we consider derivatives of the product and quotient of two functions $u(x)$ and $v(x)$. The derivative of the product uv is given by

$$\frac{d}{dx}[uv] = u\frac{dv}{dx} + v\frac{du}{dx} = u(x)v'(x) + v(x)u'(x) \tag{2.40}$$

As an example of the use of Eq. (2.40), suppose that

$$u(x) = x^2; v(x) = e^x$$

and we wish to find the derivative of the function $x^2 e^x$. Then

$$\frac{d}{dx}[x^2 e^x] = x^2 \frac{d}{dx}[e^x] + e^x \frac{d}{dx}[x^2]$$

Using Eqs. (2.37) and (2.35) we have

$$\frac{d}{dx}[e^x] = e^x; \frac{d}{dx}[x^2] = 2x$$

so

$$\frac{d}{dx}[x^2 e^x] = x^2[e^x] + e^x[2x] = e^x(x^2 + 2x) \tag{2.41}$$

The derivative of the quotient (u/v) is given by

$$\frac{d}{dx}\left[\frac{u}{v}\right] = \left(\frac{1}{v^2}\right)\left[v\frac{du}{dx} - u\frac{dv}{dx}\right] = \left(\frac{1}{v^2}\right)[v(x)u'(x) - u(x)v'(x)] \tag{2.42}$$

To illustrate the use of Eq. (2.42), let us calculate the derivative of $\tan x$ by using the trigonometric identity

$$\tan x = \frac{\sin x}{\cos x}$$

26 CALCULUS FOR PHYSICS

Then

$$\frac{d}{dx}[\tan x] = \frac{d}{dx}\left[\frac{\sin x}{\cos x}\right] \tag{2.43}$$

We evaluate Eq. (2.43) by using Eq. (2.42) with $u(x) = \sin x$ and $v(x) = \cos x$, so we obtain

$$\frac{d}{dx}\left[\frac{\sin x}{\cos x}\right] = \left(\frac{1}{\cos^2 x}\right)\left[\cos x \frac{d}{dx}[\sin x] - \sin x \frac{d}{dx}[\cos x]\right] \tag{2.44}$$

Using Eqs. (2.38) and (2.39) for the derivatives of sin x and cos x, Eq. (2.44) becomes

$$\frac{d}{dx}\left[\frac{\sin x}{\cos x}\right] = \left(\frac{1}{\cos^2 x}\right)[\cos x(\cos x) - \sin x(-\sin x)]$$

$$= \frac{1}{\cos^2 x}[\cos^2 x + \sin^2 x] = \frac{1}{\cos^2 x} = \sec^2 x \tag{2.45}$$

on using the trigonometric identity $\sin^2 x + \cos^2 x = 1$. Our final result, combining Eq. (2.43) with Eq. (2.45), is

$$\frac{d}{dx}[\tan x] = \sec^2 x \tag{2.46}$$

a result which is probably familiar to you from your calculus course. Finally, the derivative of the natural logarithm function ln x is

$$\frac{d}{dx}[\ln x] = \frac{1}{x} \tag{2.47}$$

Exercises

2.3 Calculate the derivative of the function
$$f(x) = e^x \sin x$$

2.4 Calculate the derivative of the function $f(x) = \cot x$ using the trigonometric identity
$$\cot x = \frac{\cos x}{\sin x}$$

2.5 Use Eq. (2.35) to calculate the derivatives of x^3 and x^{-1}; compare these results with those you obtained in Exercises 2.1 and 2.2 and note that they are the same.

THE CHAIN RULE. THE SECOND DERIVATIVE

Suppose a variable y is a function g of a variable u, and, further, u is itself a function f of another variable x. In equations,

$$y = g(u); \quad u = f(x) \tag{2.48}$$

Then the *chain rule* allows us to calculate the derivative $y'(x)$ of y with respect to x. The chain rule states that

$$y'(x) = g'(u)u'(x) \qquad (2.49)$$

Eq. (2.49) says that the derivative $y'(x)$ of y with respect to x is equal to the derivative $g'(u)$ of g *with respect to u* times the derivative $u'(x)$ of u with respect to x.

Let's consider an example in which

$$y = g(u) = \sin u \qquad (2.50)$$
$$u = f(x) = 2x \qquad (2.51)$$

so the function

$$y(x) = \sin 2x \qquad (2.52)$$

We want to calculate $y'(x)$, the derivative of $y(x) = \sin 2x$ with respect to x. According to the chain rule in Eq. (2.49), we need to know

$$g'(u) = \cos u \qquad (2.53)$$

and

$$u'(x) = 2 \qquad (2.54)$$

so the chain rule in Eq. (2.49) gives us

$$y'(x) = \frac{d}{dx}[\sin 2x] = (\cos u)(2) \qquad (2.55)$$

Since, from Eq. (2.51), $u = 2x$, we obtain from Eq. (2.55) the result that

$$y'(x) = \frac{d}{dx}[\sin 2x] = 2\cos 2x \qquad (2.56)$$

for the derivative of $y(x) = \sin 2x$ with respect to x.

We can see that the chain rule enables us to find the derivative of "a function of a function." Eq. (2.52) says that the variable y is a function (the sine) of the function $2x$, and, using the chain rule, we found its derivative given in Eq. (2.56).

A second example is the following, in which we find $y(x)$, take its derivative directly, and compare it with the result of using the chain rule. Suppose

$$y = g(u) = 4u^2 \qquad (2.57)$$
$$u = f(x) = 2x - 1 \qquad (2.58)$$

so

$$y(x) = f(2x - 1)^2 = 16x^2 - 16x + 4 \qquad (2.59)$$

28 CALCULUS FOR PHYSICS

Taking the derivative directly, we have
$$y'(x) = 32x - 16 \qquad (2.60)$$
Let's use the chain rule to obtain the same result. From Eqs. (2.57) and (2.58),
$$g'(u) = 8u$$
$$u'(x) = 2$$
so Eq. (2.49) for the chain rule gives us
$$y'(x) = g'(u)u'(x) = 16u \qquad (2.61)$$
Since $u = 2x - 1$, we obtain from Eq. (2.61) the result that
$$y'(x) = \frac{d}{dx}\left[4(2x-1)^2\right] = 16(2x-1) = 32x - 16 \qquad (2.62)$$
in agreement with the result in Eq. (2.60) of calculating the derivative directly.

Another example is the function
$$y(x) = \cos(6x^2) \qquad (2.63)$$
so we have, in the notation of Eqs. (2.47) to (2.49),
$$y = g(u) = \cos u$$
$$u = f(x) = 6x^2$$
From Eq. (2.49) for the chain rule,
$$y'(x) = \frac{d}{dx}\left[\cos(6x^2)\right] = g'(u)u'(x)$$
where
$$g'(u) = -\sin u$$
$$u'(x) = 12x$$
so
$$\frac{d}{dx}\left[\cos(6x^2)\right] = (-12x)\sin(6x^2) \qquad (2.64)$$
As a last example, consider the exponential function
$$y(x) = e^{ax} \qquad (2.65)$$
where a is a constant. Here $y = g(u) = e^u$ and $u = ax$, so
$$y'(x) = \frac{d}{dx}[e^{ax}] = g'(u)u'(x) = (e^u)(a)$$

so

$$\frac{d}{dx}[e^{ax}] = ae^{ax} \qquad (2.66)$$

is the derivative of e^{ax} with respect to x.

As a final point on the chain rule, it is instructive to rewrite Eq. (2.49) in a different notation as

$$\frac{dy}{dx} = \left(\frac{dy}{du}\right)\left(\frac{du}{dx}\right) \qquad (2.67)$$

where, as before in Eq. (2.48),

$$y = g(u)$$
$$u = f(x) \qquad (2.48)$$

saying y is a function g of the variable u and u is a function f of the variable x. Then Eq. (2.67), which is equivalent to Eq. (2.49), says that the derivative (dy/dx) of y with respect to x is equal to the product of the derivative (dy/du) of y, with respect to the variable u, times the derivative (du/dx) of u with respect to x. Eqs. (2.67) and (2.49) both say the same thing and both express the chain rule.

The last topic we will review here is the second derivative of a function $f(x)$. Consider the derivative $f'(x)$, where, from Eq. (2.27),

$$f'(x) = \frac{d}{dx}[f(x)] \qquad (2.27)$$

We saw, in numerous examples earlier, that the derivative $f'(x)$ is often a function of x, so we may take the derivative of the derivative $f'(x)$. We symbolize this process by

$$\frac{d}{dx}[f'(x)] = f''(x) \qquad (2.68)$$

where the symbol $f''(x)$ stands for the derivative, with respect to x, of the derivative $f'(x)$. The quantity $f''(x)$ is called the *second derivative* of the function $f(x)$. The derivative $f'(x)$ is often called the first derivative of $f(x)$.

As an example, consider the function

$$y = f(x) = x^4 \qquad (2.69)$$

whose first derivative is

$$f'(x) = 4x^3 \qquad (2.70)$$

Since $f'(x)$ is itself a function of x, we may take its derivative, obtaining the second derivative

$$f''(x) = 12x^2 \qquad (2.71)$$

(We could also differentiate $f''(x)$ and obtain the third derivative $f'''(x) = 24x$, but derivatives of order higher than the second are not of great importance in elementary physics.)

We noted earlier that, given a function

$$y = f(x) \tag{2.72}$$

the symbols

$$\frac{dy}{dx} = \frac{d}{dx}[f(x)] = \frac{df}{dx} = f'(x) \tag{2.73}$$

all are used to represent the first derivative $f'(x)$. Similarly, the second derivative $f''(x)$ of the function given by Eq. (2.72) is often represented by the symbols

$$f''(x) = \frac{d}{dx}\left[\frac{dy}{dx}\right] = \frac{d^2y}{dx^2} \tag{2.74}$$

or

$$f''(x) = \frac{d}{dx}\left[\frac{df}{dx}\right] = \frac{d^2f}{dx^2} \tag{2.75}$$

All of the symbols in Eqs. (2.74) and (2.75) mean the same thing, namely, the second derivative of the function $y = f(x)$ with respect to x. In fact, one also sees the symbol

$$\frac{d^2}{dx^2}[f(x)] = f''(x) \tag{2.76}$$

where the symbol

$$\frac{d^2}{dx^2} \tag{2.77}$$

indicates the operation of taking the second derivative of the function $f(x)$, just as the symbol

$$\frac{d}{dx} \tag{2.78}$$

in Eq. (2.27) indicated the operation of taking the first derivative.

We can illustrate the notation using our previous example

$$y = f(x) = x^4 \tag{2.69}$$

where

$$\frac{d^2y}{dx^2} = \frac{d^2f}{dx^2} = 12x^2 \tag{2.79}$$

is the second derivative of x^4 with respect to x. You will see in your physics course that the second derivative occurs in many important equations of physics.

This concludes our review of the definition of the derivative and of calculation of derivatives of various functions. We now move on to the central topic of this chapter, the meaning of the derivative as applied to physics.

Exercises

2.6 Calculate the derivative of the function
$$y(x) = e^{-2x^2}$$
2.7 Calculate the derivative of the function
$$y(x) = (x^2 + 3x - 2)^4$$
2.8 Calculate the derivative of the function
$$y(x) = \sin[e^{x^2}]$$
2.9 Given the function $y = e^x \sin x$. Calculate $f''(x)$.

RATE OF CHANGE

Let us consider a function $f(x)$ of the independent variable x where y is the dependent variable, so
$$y = f(x) \tag{2.80}$$
Since the functional relationship in Eq. (2.80) assigns a value of y to every value of x, we expect that a change in the value of x will produce a change in the value of y. Suppose that x has the value x_1, so
$$x = x_1 \tag{2.81}$$
and that x changes, by an amount Δx, to the value
$$x = x_1 + \Delta x \tag{2.82}$$
In Eq. (2.82), the amount Δx by which x changes is called the increment in x, just as it was in the earlier discussion of Eq. (2.2). When $x = x_1$, the function f has the value $f(x_1)$; when $x = (x_1 + \Delta x)$, the function f has the value $f(x_1 + \Delta x)$. Thus, when x changes from the value x_1 to the value $(x_1 + \Delta x)$, the function f changes by the amount
$$f(x_1 + \Delta x) - f(x_1) \tag{2.83}$$

32 CALCULUS FOR PHYSICS

Since, from Eq. (2.80), $y = f(x)$, the expression (2.83) is the change in the variable y when x changes from x_1 to $(x_1 + \Delta x)$. We will use the symbol Δy for this change in y, so

$$\Delta y = f(x_1 + \Delta x) - f(x_1) \tag{2.84}$$

Keep in mind that the symbol Δy, called the increment in y, is a single symbol (like the symbol Δx), and is not the product of Δ and y. Eq. (2.84) thus gives the change in the variable y when the variable x changes, by an amount Δx, from x_1 to $(x_1 + \Delta x)$. We next form the ratio of Δy to Δx,

$$\frac{\Delta y}{\Delta x} = \frac{f(x_1 + \Delta x) - f(x_1)}{\Delta x} \tag{2.85}$$

In Eq. (2.85), the ratio $(\Delta y / \Delta x)$ is called the average *rate of change* of y with respect to x. The average rate of change $(\Delta y / \Delta x)$ gives the change in y per unit of change in x, meaning that *each unit* of change in x results in a change $(\Delta y / \Delta x)$ in y. Stated again, when x changes by one unit, y changes by $(\Delta y / \Delta x)$ units. Keep in mind that we are referring only to what occurs to y when x changes by Δx over the interval from x_1 to $(x_1 + \Delta x)$, and that $(\Delta y / \Delta x)$ is the average rate of change in that interval.

Let's consider an example. Suppose

$$y = f(x) = 2x \tag{2.86}$$

is the function f, and suppose x changes from the value

$$x_1 = 2.00 \tag{2.87}$$

to the value

$$x_1 + \Delta x = 2.01 \tag{2.88}$$

so the increment in x is $\Delta x = 0.01$. We want to calculate first the increment Δy in y. Since $f(x) = 2x$, we have

$$f(x_1) = 2(2.00) = 4.00$$

$$f(x_1 + \Delta x) = 2(2.01) = 4.02$$

$$\Delta y = f(x_1 + \Delta x) - f(x_1) = 4.02 - 4.00 = 0.02 \tag{2.89}$$

Forming the ratio $(\Delta y / \Delta x)$, we obtain

$$\frac{\Delta y}{\Delta x} = \frac{f(x_1 + \Delta x) - f(x_1)}{\Delta x} = \frac{0.02}{0.01} = 2 \tag{2.90}$$

Eq. (2.90) gives the value of $(\Delta y / \Delta x)$, the average rate of change of y with respect to x over the interval $\Delta x = 0.01$ from $x = 2.00$ to

$x = 2.01$. We can rewrite Eq. (2.90) as

$$\Delta y = 2(\Delta x) \qquad (2.91)$$

an equation which tells us that the increment or change Δy in y is twice the increment or change Δx in x. Thus we see again the meaning of the rate of change $(\Delta y/\Delta x)$ in Eq. (2.90); it gives the change in y per unit of change in x. When x changes by one unit, y changes by two units, so the rate of change of y with respect to x has the value 2.

We can use these results to calculate, for example, the change Δy in y when x changes from $x_1 = 2.000$ to $(x_1 + \Delta x) = 2.005$, so $\Delta x = 0.005$. Since $(\Delta y/\Delta x) = 2$ is the average rate of change of y with respect to x for values of x between 2.00 and 2.01, we can use the value $(\Delta y/\Delta x) = 2$ to find Δy when $\Delta x = 0.005$. Using Eq. (2.91), we have

$$\Delta y = 2(\Delta x) = 2(0.005) = 0.01 \qquad (2.92)$$

so y changes by the increment $\Delta y = 0.01$ when x changes by the increment $\Delta x = 0.005$ when x changes from 2.000 to 2.005.

So far we haven't specified any *physical meaning* to the variables x and y connected by the functional relation $y = f(x)$ in Eq. (2.80). They can just be considered as mathematical variables, but, for concreteness, let's consider a physical example. Suppose x is a horizontal distance, measured in meters, and y is a vertical distance, also in meters, and suppose further that y is a function of x as in Eq. (2.86), which says

$$y = f(x) = 2x \qquad (2.86)$$

The variables x and y might be related to a ski run whose constant steepness is such that, as in Fig. 2.1, the vertical distance y is twice the

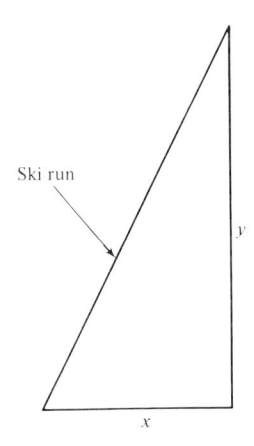

Figure 2.1 Vertical distance y and horizontal distance x for a ski run.

horizontal distance x. Then, as we found before,

$$\frac{\Delta y}{\Delta x} = 2 \tag{2.93}$$

is the average rate of change of y (vertical distance) with respect to x (horizontal distance). Skiing down the run, the skier would move a vertical distance (in meters) of $(\Delta y / \Delta x) = 2$ for each meter of horizontal distance moved. Since

$$\Delta y = 2(\Delta x) \tag{2.94}$$

the skier would, for instance, move a vertical distance $\Delta y = 10$ meters while moving a horizontal distance $\Delta x = 5$ meters.

Exercises

2.10 Given the function $y = 6x + 2$, (a) Calculate the average rate of change of y with respect to x over the interval from $x = 1.00$ to $x = 1.01$; (b) Calculate the change Δy in y when x changes from 1.00 to 1.01.

CONNECTION BETWEEN THE DERIVATIVE AND RATE OF CHANGE

In the preceding section, the quantity

$$\frac{\Delta y}{\Delta x} = \frac{f(x_1 + \Delta x) - f(x_1)}{\Delta x} \tag{2.95}$$

was introduced as the average rate of change of y, with respect to x, over the interval Δx from x_1 to $(x_1 + \Delta x)$. We now let Δx become very small and take the limit

$$\lim_{\Delta x \to 0} \frac{f(x_1 + \Delta x) - f(x_1)}{\Delta x} = f'(x_1) \tag{2.96}$$

using the definition of the derivative in Eq. (2.7). Eq. (2.96) is the derivative $f'(x_1)$ of the function $f(x)$ at the point $x = x_1$. Since the expression in Eq. (2.95) is a rate of change, it is reasonable to expect that the derivative $f'(x_1)$ given by Eq. (2.96) will also be a rate of change.

Since the quantity given by Eq. (2.95) is the average rate of change of y with respect to x, and since also

$$y = f(x) \tag{2.97}$$

we may say also that the quantity

$$\frac{f(x_1 + \Delta x) - f(x_1)}{\Delta x} \tag{2.98}$$

is the average rate of change of the function $f(x)$, with respect to x, over the interval Δx from x_1 to $(x_1 + \Delta x)$. When the limit as $\Delta x \to 0$ is taken in Eq. (2.96), we are essentially finding the average rate of change of $f(x)$ over smaller and smaller intervals of size Δx from x_1 to $(x_1 + \Delta x)$. We know, from the definition of the derivative in Eq. (2.96), that the limit approached by Eq. (2.98) is $f'(x_1)$, the derivative at $x = x_1$. As we take the limit of expression (2.98) as $\Delta x \to 0$, the *average* rate of change of the function $f(x)$ approaches $f'(x_1)$ as its limiting value. We call this limiting value $f'(x_1)$ the *instantaneous* rate of change of $f(x)$, with respect to x, at the point $x = x_1$.

We may restate this conclusion for emphasis. As the limit as $\Delta x \to 0$ is taken, the average rate of change of $f(x)$, given by Eq. (2.98), approaches $f'(x_1)$, the value of the derivative at $x = x_1$. The derivative $f'(x_1)$, at $x = x_1$, is the instantaneous rate of change of $f(x)$, with respect to x, at the point $x = x_1$.

Let's consider again the example in the previous section. We recall that the function was

$$y = f(x) = 2x \tag{2.86}$$

and we found in Eq. (2.90) that the average rate of change of y, or f, was, for $x_1 = 2$,

$$\frac{f(x_1 + \Delta x) - f(x_1)}{\Delta x} = 2 \tag{2.90}$$

From Eq. (2.86), we calculate that

$$f'(x) = \frac{d}{dx}(2x) = 2 \tag{2.99}$$

is the derivative of $f(x) = 2x$, with respect to x, for *any* value of x, including, of course, $x = x_1 = 2$. The derivative $f'(x)$ thus has the value 2 for $x = x_1 = 2$, so

$$f'(x_1) = f'(2) = 2 \tag{2.100}$$

is the value of the derivative of $f(x) = 2x$ for $x = 2$. The value of the *instantaneous* rate of change of the function $f(x) = 2x$ therefore has the value 2 for all values of x.

As another example, consider

$$y = f(x) = 2x^2 \tag{2.101}$$

so

$$f'(x) = 4x \tag{2.102}$$

The derivative $f'(x)$ in Eq. (2.102) is itself a function of x, so the value of $f'(x)$ will vary with the value of x. When x has the value x_1, the derivative has the value

$$f'(x_1) = 4x_1 \qquad (2.103)$$

From the preceding discussion, we see that $f'(x_1) = 4x_1$ is the value of the instantaneous rate of change of the function $f(x) = 2x^2$ at the value $x = x_1$. For example, if $x_1 = 3$, the value of the derivative is

$$f'(x_1) = f'(3) = 4(3) = 12 \qquad (2.104)$$

so the instantaneous rate of change of $f(x) = 2x^2$, with respect to x, is the value $f'(3) = 12$ when $x = 3$.

What does the word "instantaneous" mean when we say "instantaneous rate of change of $f(x)$ with respect to x?" The dictionary definition of instantaneous is "occurring or present at a specific instant of time." Since time is not involved here (that will come later), we will take instantaneous to mean "for a particular value of the independent variable." Thus, the derivative $f'(x_1)$ is the instantaneous rate of change of the function $f(x)$ for the value $x = x_1$ of the independent variable x. As an example, consider the function $f(x) = 2x^2$, given in Eq. (2.101), for which the derivative $f'(x) = 4x$ is the instantaneous rate of change. This means that the instantaneous rate of change of the function $f(x) = 2x^2$ is the quantity $f'(x) = 4x$, which itself depends on x. Hence, in this case, the value of the instantaneous rate of change depends on the value of the independent

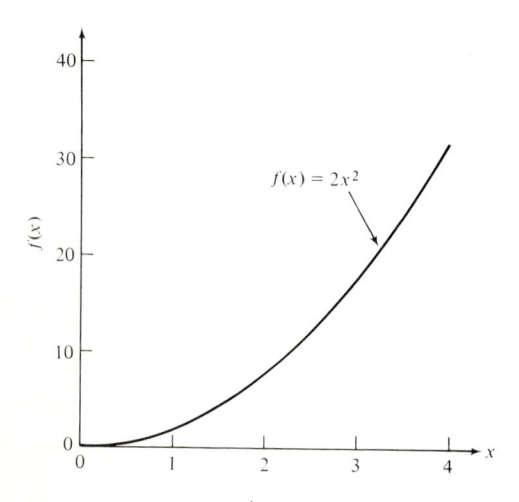

Figure 2.2 Graph of $f(x) = 2x^2$ as a function of x.

variable x. As shown in Eq. (2.104),

$$f'(3) = 4(3) = 12 \tag{2.105}$$

is the value of the instantaneous rate of change of $f(x) = 2x^2$ for the value $x = 3$ of the independent variable x. For, say, $x = 4$,

$$f'(4) = 4(4) = 16 \tag{2.106}$$

so the instantaneous rate of change $f'(4)$ has the value 16 when $x = 4$.

We can visualize these results by making graphs of $f(x) = 2x^2$ and $f'(x) = 4x$; these are shown in Figs. 2.2 and 2.3, respectively. Fig. 2.3 shows the derivative $f'(x) = 4x$ plotted as a function of x. We can read values of $f'(x)$ for any value of x off the graph. The values $f'(3) = 12$ for $x = 3$ and $f'(4) = 16$ for $x = 4$ are shown on the graph. Note that the graph of the equation $f'(x) = 4x$ shows explicitly that the derivative is a function of x.

We may extend this idea as follows. Since $f'(x_1)$ is the instantaneous rate of change of $f(x)$ for $x = x_1$, and x_1 may be *any* value of x, the derivative $f'(x)$ is referred to as the instantaneous rate of change of $f(x)$ with respect to x. The derivative $f'(x)$ will usually be a function of x, so the value of the instantaneous rate of change will generally depend on x. Thus, using our earlier example, if $f(x) = 2x^2$,

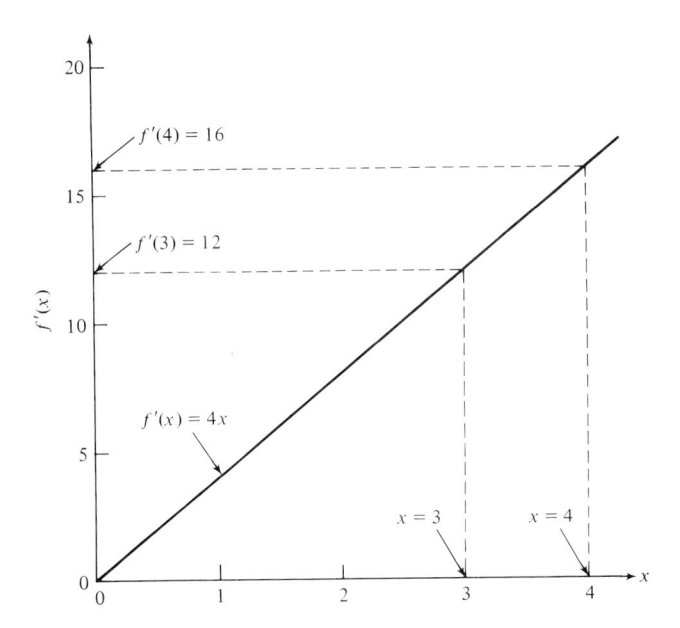

Figure 2.3 Graph of $f'(x) = 4x$ as a function of x.

the derivative $f'(x) = 4x$ is the instantaneous rate of change of $f(x)$ with respect to x. The value of $f'(x)$ depends on x and will have different values for different values of x. For example, $f'(4) = 16$ is the value of the instantaneous rate of change of $f(x) = 2x^2$ for the value $x = 4$ of the independent variable x.

It is useful to summarize briefly the results obtained so far. Given the function $f(x)$, the derivative $f'(x)$ is called the instantaneous rate of change of $f(x)$ with respect to x. The value $f'(x_1)$ of the derivative for $x = x_1$ is the value of that rate of change when $x = x_1$.

We defer the discussion of the *meaning* of the instantaneous rate of change to the next section.

Exercises

2.11 Given the function $y = f(x) = x^3$. (a) Calculate the instantaneous rate of change of $f(x)$ with respect to x; (b) Calculate the value of this rate of change when $x = 1$.

MEANING OF INSTANTANEOUS RATE OF CHANGE. FUNCTIONS OF TIME

The meaning of the instantaneous rate of change of a function is most clearly explained by considering functions which vary with the *time*. We are all familiar with quantities which are functions of time. Common examples are the temperature of the air and the distance moved by an auto.

We will use the latter example in order to discuss in detail the meaning of the instantaneous rate of change of a function. Suppose we consider an auto starting from rest and moving in a straight line, and suppose further that we know the distance moved as a function of time. We will use the symbols s for distance and t for time, so we know distance s as a function of time t, which we write as

$$s = f(t) \qquad (2.107)$$

In Eq. (2.107), s is the distance moved from the starting point and t is the elapsed time after the auto starts to move. Eq. (2.107) allows us, in principle, to calculate the distance the auto has moved during any elapsed time. We will usually measure distance in meters and time in seconds.

It is useful to digress briefly here to explain in detail the precise meanings of distance and time as used in Eq. (2.107) or others like it. The symbol s refers to the distance moved, measured from the starting point. For example, if the car at some point on its path has moved 1000 meters from the starting position, we would say that $s = 1000$ meters. The position or point from which the distance is measured is often called the zero point or the zero of distance because it is the point at which $s = 0$. Since s is the distance *moved*, $s = 0$ at the starting point. The symbol t refers to elapsed time, as measured from the instant at which the motion begins. (Note that t is *not* a clock time like, say, 11:15 A.M.). For example, if we were considering an instant of time 30 seconds after the car starts moving, we would say that $t = 30$ seconds at that instant. Since t is the elapsed time, $t = 0$ at the instant the motion begins. To summarize these points, distance s is measured from the starting point of the motion and time t is measured from the starting time of the motion. At the instant at which the motion begins, $s = 0$ and $t = 0$, and both s and t increase as the motion proceeds with time.

We return to Eq. (2.107) giving the distance moved as a function of time,

$$s = f(t) \qquad (2.107)$$

The derivative of $f(t)$ is, from the definition,

$$\frac{ds}{dt} = f'(t) = \lim_{\Delta t \to 0} \frac{f(t + \Delta t) - f(t)}{\Delta t} \qquad (2.108)$$

In Eq. (2.108), $f(t)$ is the distance moved at the instant of time t, $f(t + \Delta t)$ is the distance moved at the later instant of time $(t + \Delta t)$, and Δt is the length of the time interval between those two instants. Since the quantity

$$f(t + \Delta t) - f(t)$$

is the distance moved in the time interval of length Δt, we can see that

$$\frac{f(t + \Delta t) - f(t)}{\Delta t}$$

is the average rate of change of distance with time during the time interval of length Δt. When we take the limit, as $\Delta t \to 0$, in Eq. (2.108), we obtain the derivative $f'(t)$ of distance s with respect to time t. From our results in the preceding section, the derivative $(ds/dt) = f'(t)$ is the instantaneous rate of change of distance with respect to time. We will discuss this particular rate of change in detail as a way of introducing and illuminating the general idea of an instantaneous rate of change.

For concreteness, let us consider as an example the specific function

$$s = f(t) = 2t^2 \qquad (2.109)$$

40 CALCULUS FOR PHYSICS

giving the distance s moved by the auto as a function of time t. The derivative

$$\frac{ds}{dt} = f'(t) = 4t \qquad (2.110)$$

is the instantaneous rate of change of distance with respect to time when the distance is given as a function of time by Eq. (2.109).

The physical meaning of the rate of change of distance with respect to time is familiar to us as *velocity*. Velocity, commonly expressed in units like miles per hour or meters per second, means the distance moved in one unit of time, often called the distance moved per unit time. Each of the quantities given in Eq. (2.110) is the *instantaneous velocity* of the auto, meaning the auto's velocity at one instant of time. If distance s is expressed in meters and time in seconds in Eq. (2.109), then the instantaneous velocity will be in meters per second. Eq. (2.110) therefore gives the instantaneous velocity, which is the instantaneous rate of change of distance with respect to time. We can write

$$v \equiv \frac{ds}{dt} = f'(t) \qquad (2.111)$$

defining the instantaneous velocity v as the instantaneous rate of change of distance s with respect to time t. Since in this example, $f'(t) = 4t$, we have

$$v = \frac{ds}{dt} = f'(t) = 4t \qquad (2.112)$$

an equation which gives the instantaneous velocity v as a function of time.

The velocity itself varies with time and we may, from Eq. (2.112), calculate v at any instant of time. For example, if we consider the instant of time 4 seconds after the auto starts, we are considering the instant when

$$t = 4 \text{ seconds} \qquad (2.113)$$

Substituting $t = 4$ seconds into Eq. (2.112), we obtain

$$v = f'(4) = 4(4) = 16 \text{ meters per second} \qquad (2.114)$$

giving the value $v = 16$ meters per second of the instantaneous velocity v at the particular instant of time $t = 4$ seconds.

We digress briefly again here to consider the notation used to indicate the value of the derivative at a particular instant or value of the time. Considering a function $f(x)$ of x, we have been using the notation $f'(x_1)$ to indicate the value of the derivative $f'(x)$ at the particular point $x = x_1$. There is another common notation in use. If (dy/dx) is the derivative of $y = f(x)$ with respect to x, then the symbol

$$\left(\frac{dy}{dx}\right)_{x=x_1} \tag{2.115}$$

is also used to indicate the value of the derivative at the point $x = x_1$. One might also see

$$\left(\frac{df}{dx}\right)_{x=x_1} \tag{2.116}$$

for the same derivative evaluated at $x = x_1$. All three notations are equivalent, so if we consider a function $y = f(x)$, it is true that

$$\left(\frac{dy}{dx}\right)_{x=x_1} = \left(\frac{df}{dx}\right)_{x=x_1} = f'(x_1) \tag{2.117}$$

all of which mean the value of the derivative at the point $x = x_1$. Applying this notation to functions of time, we indicate the value of the derivative $f'(t)$ when $t = 4$ seconds by any of the following symbols,

$$\left(\frac{ds}{dt}\right)_{t=4} = \left(\frac{df}{dt}\right)_{t=4} = f'(4) \tag{2.118}$$

all of which mean the same thing: the derivative of distance s, with respect to time t, evaluated at the particular instant of time $t = 4$ seconds.

Returning to our consideration of the derivative of distance with respect to time, we note particularly the use of the term "instantaneous" in the discussion of velocity. We earlier defined the instantaneous rate of change as the rate of change for a particular value of the independent variable. Thus $f'(x)$ is the instantaneous rate of change of $f(x)$ for some particular value of x. In treating velocity, we are dealing with distance as a function of the independent variable time. The instantaneous velocity is the instantaneous rate of change of distance, with respect to time, for some particular value of time, so $v = (ds/dt) = f'(t)$ is the value of the velocity for a particular value of the time.

We can visualize how the instantaneous velocity changes with time by making a graph of Eq. (2.112) giving v as a function of time. Fig. 2.4 shows a graph of the equation

$$v = f'(t) = 4t \tag{2.119}$$

42 CALCULUS FOR PHYSICS

as a function of time, for times from 0 to 5 seconds. The instantaneous velocity v is plotted in meters per second and time t is in seconds. We can see from the graph that the instantaneous velocity v increases with time from the value $v = 0$ when $t = 0$ (the auto starts from rest at $t = 0$) to the value $v = 20$ meters per second when $t = 5$ seconds.

Since the velocity is the instantaneous rate of change of distance with respect to time, the graph in Fig. 2.4 shows clearly that *the rate of change is itself changing with time*. The instantaneous rate of change is just the value of the rate of change at some particular instant of time. On the graph is shown the value $v = 16$ meters per second of the instantaneous rate of change (velocity), at the instant $t = 4$ seconds, as given by the relations in Eq. (2.114).

We may now summarize our results concerning the instantaneous velocity. Given the distance s moved as a function of elapsed time t, as

$$s = f(t) \tag{2.120}$$

Then the instantaneous rate of change of distance with respect to time t is called the instantaneous velocity v, so

$$v = \frac{ds}{dt} = f'(t) \tag{2.121}$$

In general the velocity v will vary with time, so the rate of change $f'(t)$ is itself a function of time and varies with time. The instantaneous

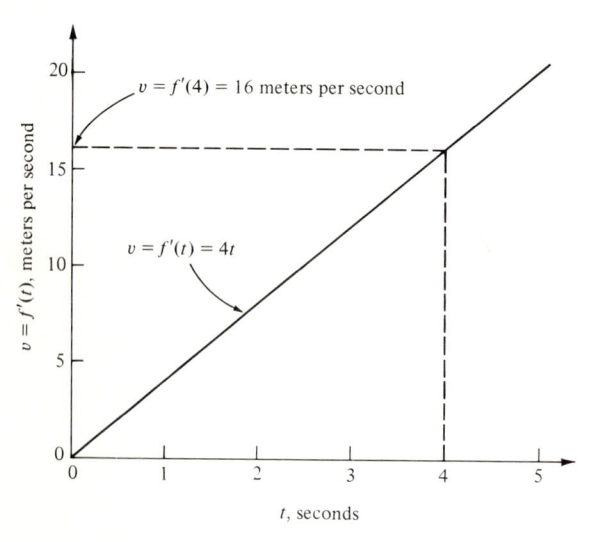

Figure 2.4 Instantaneous velocity $v = f'(t)$ as a function of time t when $v = f'(t) = 4t$.

velocity v, or instantaneous rate of change $f'(t)$, is then the value at some particular value of t, i.e., at some particular instant of time.

We can now see the general meaning of an instantaneous rate of change. Given a function $f(x)$, then $f'(x)$ is the instantaneous rate of change of $f(x)$ with respect to x. In general, the rate of change $f'(x)$ will itself be a function of the independent variable x. The instantaneous rate of change thus specifies the rate of change for some particular value of x. While we have illustrated the idea of an instantaneous rate of change with the example of velocity, there are many other quantities in physics whose rates of change with respect to some independent variable are of interest. Often the independent variable of interest in physics is the time, but that is not always the case. We now examine some examples of rates of change, including one with respect to a variable other than the time.

As an example of a rate of change, let's consider the familiar phenomenon of the variation of the temperature of some object with time. Suppose a sample of water is heated and the temperature T (in kelvins, K) is measured as a function of time t (in seconds). Suppose further that the temperature as a function $f(t)$ of time is found to be

$$T = f(t) = 0.5t + 300 \qquad (2.122)$$

an equation in which the temperature T is the dependent variable and the time t is the independent variable. Then the derivative $f'(t)$ is the instantaneous rate of change of the temperature T with respect to time t. Differentiating T with respect to t in Eq. (2.122) yields

$$f'(t) = \frac{dT}{dt} = 0.5 \qquad (2.123)$$

Eq. (2.123) gives us (dT/dt), the instantaneous rate of change of temperature with respect to time as 0.5 kelvins per second. This rate of change is the change in temperature per unit of change in time. In this example, the rate of change is 0.5 kelvins in 1 second and the rate of change is constant and does not itself vary with the time.

Let us consider as a second example one in which the rate of change is *not* with respect to time. Consider the situation shown in Fig. 2.5, in which we have a thin rod of metal with its length oriented parallel to the x axis. Let us choose the origin $x = 0$ at the left-hand end (1) of the rod; then, if the rod is of length 1 m, the right-hand end (2) will be at the point $x = 1$ meter on the x-axis. Suppose that the left-hand end (1) is heated, so heat flows along the rod from end (1) to end (2). Suppose also that we have measured the temperature T at many points between $x = 0$ and $x = 1$, so we know the temperature as a function $f(x)$ of position along the rod between $x = 0$ and $x = 1$. As an equation, we have

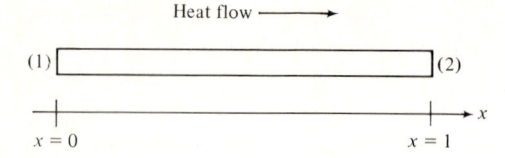

$$T = f(x) \tag{2.124}$$

giving the dependent variable T as a function of distance x [measured from $x = 0$ at the end (1) of the rod] along the rod. As a concrete example, suppose

$$T = f(x) = 400 - 100x \tag{2.125}$$

where T is in kelvins (K) and x is in meters (m). Since the temperature varies along the length of the rod, there will be a rate of change of temperature T *with respect to distance* x along the rod. The derivative $f'(x)$ of T with respect to x is the instantaneous rate of change (in kelvins per meter) of temperature with respect to distance. Calculating the derivative $f'(x)$ from Eq. (2.125) gives the result

$$f'(x) = \frac{dT}{dx} = -100 \tag{2.126}$$

Eq. (2.126) gives (dT/dx), the instantaneous rate of change of temperature, with respect to distance, as -100 kelvins per meter. The negative sign means that the temperature is decreasing with increasing distance, meaning that the temperature is lower at points further away from the left-hand end of the rod at $x = 0$. The rate of change is the change in temperature per unit of change of distance. In this example, that rate of change is (-100) kelvins in one meter, and, again, the rate of change is constant and does not itself vary with distance along the rod. The derivative (dT/dx) is called the temperature gradient along the length of the rod.

Exercises

2.12 It is found in a certain physics experiment that the distance s moved by a body is directly proportional to the cube of the time t the body moves. (a) Using the symbol B for the constant of proportionality, write the equation giving s as a function of t; (b) Use your result in Part (a) to find the rate of change of distance with respect to time. (c) Write down an expression for the velocity of the body as a function of time.

2.13 Starting from rest, a block of ice slides down a chute in such a way that the distance s that it moves is given as a function of time t by the relation

$$s = 2.4t^2$$

where s is in meters if t is in seconds. (a) Find the equation giving the rate of change of distance with respect to time; (b) Is the rate of change found in Part (a) a function of time? (c) Calculate the velocity of the ice block 1 second after it begins to move.

2.14 The circumference C of a circle is given as a function of its radius r by the equation

$$C = 2\pi r$$

(a) Find the equation giving the rate of change of the circumference of the circle with respect to its radius; (b) Express in your own words the meaning of the rate of change in (a).

THE SECOND DERIVATIVE AND ACCELERATION

We have seen that the physical meaning of the derivative $f'(x)$ of a function $f(x)$ is the rate of change of the function $f(x)$ with respect to x. We now examine the meaning of the *second* derivative of a function. We consider again a function $f(t)$, of the time t, whose first derivative is $f'(t)$. Then the second derivative may be written in the various equivalent ways

$$f''(t) = \frac{d}{dt}[f'(t)] = \frac{d}{dt}\left[\frac{df}{dt}\right] \qquad (2.127)$$

Eq. (2.127) says that the second derivative $f''(t)$ is the derivative, with respect to time, of the derivative $f'(t)$. Since $f'(t)$ is the rate of change of $f(t)$ with respect to time, the second derivative $f''(t)$ is the rate of change, with respect to time, of the rate of change. In short, the second derivative is the rate of change of the rate of change.

We can illustrate this with a physical example by considering the velocity, given by Eq. (2.111) as

$$v = \frac{ds}{dt} = f'(t) \qquad (2.111)$$

where the distance s is a function $f(t)$ of the time. If we take the derivative with respect to time of v in Eq. (2.111), we obtain

$$\frac{dv}{dt} = \frac{d}{dt}\left(\frac{ds}{dt}\right) = \frac{d^2s}{dt^2} = f''(t) \qquad (2.128)$$

Eq. (2.128) says that the second derivative (d^2s/dt^2) of the distance, with respect to time, is equal to the rate of change of the velocity v with respect to time. Since we have seen that the velocity is itself the rate of change of distance with respect to time, the quantity (dv/dt) is

46 CALCULUS FOR PHYSICS

the rate of change of the rate of change of distance with respect to time. The rate of change (dv/dt) is called the *acceleration*, so acceleration is the rate of change of velocity with respect to time. An equivalent is that the second derivative of distance, with respect to time, is equal to the acceleration.

Let's discuss a specific example. Suppose we consider a body falling vertically from rest under the influence of gravity without any air resistance. Then it is known experimentally that the vertical distance s the body falls in time t is given by

$$s = 4.9t^2 \qquad (2.129)$$

Eq. (2.129) gives s in meters if t is in seconds. As before, t is measured from the instant at which the body starts to fall and s is measured from the starting point. Since Eq. (2.129) gives distance as a function of time, we may calculate the velocity by differentiating s with respect to t, obtaining

$$v = \frac{ds}{dt} = 9.8t \qquad (2.130)$$

Eq. (2.130) gives the velocity v as a function of the time, and shows that the velocity itself varies with the time. Since s is in meters and t is in seconds, v in Eq. (2.130) is in meters per second.

Since the acceleration is the rate of change of velocity with respect to time, we may find the acceleration (denoted by the symbol a) by differentiating v with respect to time. Using Eq. (2.130), the result is

$$a = \frac{dv}{dt} = \frac{d}{dt}\left(\frac{ds}{dt}\right) = \frac{d^2s}{dt^2} = 9.8 \qquad (2.131)$$

Eq. (2.131) says that the acceleration a has the constant value 9.8, which is in units of meters per second per second since the velocity is in meters per second. The unit of acceleration "meters per second per second" emphasizes that acceleration is the rate of change of velocity with time. The statement of Eq. (2.131) that

$$a = \frac{dv}{dt} = 9.8 \text{ meters per second per second} \qquad (2.132)$$

says that the velocity is changing with time at the constant rate of (9.8 meters per second) per second. Note that in this example the acceleration has a constant value and does not vary with the time.

Let's consider another example, one in which a particle moves along the x axis starting from the origin ($x = 0$) when the time $t = 0$. Although we have generally been using the symbol s for the distance moved, we will use x for the distance from the origin in this example. (This common usage is because the motion is confined to the x axis.) Suppose x is given as a function of time t by the equation

$$x = A \sin \omega t \qquad (2.133)$$

where A and ω are constants. Thus, Eq. (2.133) gives x, the distance of the particle from the origin at the time t, i.e., after an elapsed time t. The velocity v of the particle is the rate of change of distance x with respect to time t, so

$$v = \frac{dx}{dt} = A\omega \cos \omega t \qquad (2.134)$$

Eq. (2.134) gives the velocity v of the particle as a function of time t; v is equal to the constant $(A\omega)$ times the cosine of ωt. We see that the velocity varies cosinusoidally with the time. Next, the acceleration a of the particle is the rate of change of velocity with respect to time, so

$$a = \frac{dv}{dt} = \frac{d}{dt}[A\omega \cos \omega t] = -A\omega^2 \sin \omega t \qquad (2.135)$$

Eq. (2.135) gives the acceleration a of the particle as a function of time t: a is equal to the constant $(-A\omega^2)$ times the sine of ωt. Thus the acceleration varies sinusoidally with the time. Note that, in contrast to the preceding example, the acceleration in this case is not constant and does vary with time. The motion described by Eqs. (2.133)–(2.135) is called *simple harmonic motion* and is very common in physics.

To summarize, the second derivative is the rate of change of the rate of change. An important physical example is the acceleration, which is the second derivative of distance with respect to time. The acceleration is thus the rate of change, with respect to time, of velocity, which is itself the rate of change of distance with respect to time.

Exercises

2.15 Using your results obtained in solving Exercise 2.12, calculate the acceleration of the moving body.

DIFFERENTIALS

We now consider the differential, a concept that is used frequently in physics and which is assumed to have been discussed, but probably not extensively, in your calculus course. Suppose we have a function

$$y = f(x) \qquad (2.136)$$

of the independent variable x. We introduce the symbol dx, called the differential of x. (Note that dx is a single symbol; it does *not* mean d times x.) The differential dx may be any real number, although (as we will see later) it is usually considered to be a very small number in situations of interest in physics.

We next introduce the differential of the function $f(x)$, denoted by the symbol df, and defined by the equation

$$df \equiv f'(x)\, dx \qquad (2.137)$$

where, as usual, $f'(x)$ is the derivative of $f(x)$ with respect to x. Eq. (2.137) says that the differential df of the function $f(x)$ is equal to the product of the derivative $f'(x)$ and the differential dx of the independent variable x. Since, from Eq. (2.136), $y = f(x)$, the differential of the function $f(x)$ is also denoted by the symbol dy, so Eq. (2.137) may also be written

$$dy = f'(x)\, dx \qquad (2.138)$$

The quantity dy is a single symbol and is called the differential of y. Note that, from Eq. (2.138), the differential dy is a function of both x and dx, meaning that dy depends on the two quantities, x and dx.

As an example, consider the function

$$y = f(x) = x^3 \qquad (2.139)$$

Then the differential of y is given by

$$dy = f'(x)\, dx = (3x^2)\, dx \qquad (2.140)$$

where the parentheses in Eq. (2.140) are used to emphasize the fact that the differential dy is equal to the product of the function $3x^2$ and the differential dx. Since $y = f(x)$, we could equally well have written the result in Eq. (2.140) as

$$df = f'(x)\, dx = (3x^2)\, dx \qquad (2.141)$$

an equation which has the same content as Eq. (2.140). We will use whichever of the equivalent symbols dy or df is the more convenient in a given situation.

If we divide the differential dy as given by Eq. (2.138) by the differential dx, we obtain, assuming dx is not zero,

$$\frac{dy}{dx} = \frac{f'(x)\, dx}{dx} = f'(x) \qquad (2.142)$$

Eq. (2.142) is very important. It says that the derivative $f'(x)$, of the function $y = f(x)$, is equal to the quotient of the differential dy, of y, divided by the differential dx. As an example, we take dy for the function $y = x^3$ given by Eq. (2.140) and divide it by dx, obtaining

$$\frac{dy}{dx} = \frac{(3x^2)\,dx}{dx} = 3x^2 \tag{2.143}$$

Eq. (2.143) says that the ratio of dy to dx is equal to the quantity $3x^2$, which is, of course, the derivative of x^3.

The fact that the derivative $f'(x)$ can be expressed as the ratio of the differentials dy and dx is much used in physics. Differentials may be manipulated just like numbers and may be added, subtracted, multiplied, and divided (whenever not equal to zero). A useful instance is afforded by the chain rule which was discussed earlier. There we considered two functions

$$y = g(u); \; u = f(x) \tag{2.144}$$

and the chain rule gives the derivative $y'(x)$ of y with respect to x as

$$y'(x) = g'(u)u'(x) \tag{2.145}$$

Eq. (2.145) says that the derivative $y'(x)$ is equal to the derivative $g'(u)$ of g with respect to u times the derivative $u'(x)$ of u with respect to x. This can be written in alternative notation as

$$\frac{dy}{dx} = \left(\frac{dy}{du}\right)\left(\frac{du}{dx}\right) \tag{2.146}$$

since $g'(u) = (dy/du)$ and $u'(x) = (du/dx)$. Eq. (2.146) says that the derivative (dy/dx) is the product of the derivative (dy/du) and the derivative (du/dx). If we regard the derivatives in Eq. (2.146) as ratios of differentials, we may write the product

$$\left(\frac{dy}{du}\right)\left(\frac{du}{dx}\right) \tag{2.147}$$

and then "cancel" the differential du in the numerator and denominator, treating du just like a number. The result of "canceling" the differential du in Eq. (2.147) is shown in Eq. (2.148),

$$\left(\frac{dy}{\cancel{du}}\right)\left(\frac{\cancel{du}}{dx}\right) = \frac{dy}{dx} \tag{2.148}$$

where the diagonal lines through the differentials du indicate "cancellation." Eq. (2.148) is a statement of the chain rule for the functions involved and shows the utility of the approach using differentials.

As a specific example of the use of differentials, suppose we have the function

$$y = \sin x^3$$

50 CALCULUS FOR PHYSICS

so we have then
$$y = g(u) = \sin u$$
$$u = f(x) = x^3$$
and we want to find (dy/dx), the derivative of y with respect to x. We could do it directly with the chain rule in Eq. (2.146) by calculating the required derivatives, but let's do it instead with differentials. From the definition of the differential of a function given in Eq. (2.138), we have

$$dy = g'(u)\, du = (\cos u)\, du \qquad (2.149)$$

Let's divide both sides of Eq. (2.149) by the differential dx, obtaining

$$\frac{dy}{dx} = (\cos u)\left(\frac{du}{dx}\right) \qquad (2.150)$$

an equation that says the derivative (dy/dx) is equal to $\cos u$ times the derivative (du/dx). We can calculate (du/dx) from the differential du, given by

$$du = f'(x)\, dx = (3x^2)\, dx \qquad (2.151)$$

Then we divide both sides of Eq. (2.151) by the differential dx, obtaining

$$\frac{du}{dx} = \frac{(3x^2)\, dx}{dx} = 3x^2$$

Substituting $u = x^3$ and $(du/dx) = 3x^2$ into Eq. (2.150) gives the result

$$\frac{dy}{dx} = (3x^2)(\cos x^3)$$

for the required derivative (dy/dx). This result is, of course, the same as that obtained by applying the chain rule directly to the derivatives.

The differential can also be useful in finding rates of change of various sorts. An example would be a rate of change with respect to time. Consider the familiar equation

$$C = 2\pi r \qquad (2.152)$$

for the circumference C of a circle as a function of its radius r. Suppose we are interested in finding (dC/dt), the rate of change of the circumference with respect to time. Let us take the differential dC of C from Eq. (2.152), obtaining

$$dC = (2\pi)\, dr \qquad (2.153)$$

where dr is the differential of r. Next, we divide both sides of Eq. (2.153) by dt, the differential of t, the time. The result is

$$\frac{dC}{dt} = (2\pi)\frac{dr}{dt} \qquad (2.154)$$

Eq. (2.154) tells us that the rate of change (dC/dt) of the circumference C with respect to time t is equal to the constant 2π times the rate of change (dr/dt) of the radius r with respect to time t.

This section is concluded with a brief list of differentials of common functions. In Eq. (2.149), we saw that, if $y = \sin u$, the differential dy is given by

$$dy = (\cos u)\, du \qquad (2.155)$$

The result exhibited in Eq. (2.155) is often expressed as

$$d[\sin u] = \cos u\, du \qquad (2.156)$$

Eq. (2.156) is read "the differential of the sine of u is equal to the cosine of u times the differential du of u." Equations like Eq. (2.156) are frequently used to express the differential of some function. Just as the symbol

$$\frac{d}{dx}[f(x)]$$

was used earlier to indicate the *operation* of taking the derivative of the function f, the symbol

$$d[f(x)]$$

expresses the operation of taking the *differential* of the function f. Thus, in Eq. (2.156), $d[\sin u]$ indicates the operation of taking the differential of the function $\sin u$, and that that differential equals the cosine of u times the differential du.

This notation is used in the short list of differentials that follows; in the list u and v are functions, and a and n are constants

$$d[au] = a\, du \qquad (2.157)$$
$$d[u + v] = du + dv \qquad (2.158)$$
$$d[u^n] = (nu^{n-1})\, du \qquad (2.159)$$
$$d[e^u] = e^u\, du \qquad (2.160)$$
$$d[\ln u] = (1/u)\, du \qquad (2.161)$$
$$d[\sin u] = (\cos u)\, du \qquad (2.162)$$
$$d[\cos u] = (-\sin u)\, du \qquad (2.163)$$
$$d[uv] = u\, dv + v\, du \qquad (2.164)$$

Exercises

2.16 Given the function $y = f(x) = 6\cos 6x^4$. Find the differential dy.

2.17 Given that the area A of a circle is πr^2, where r is the radius. Calculate the rate of change of the area with respect to time. Express the meaning of your result in words.

PHYSICAL APPLICATIONS OF DIFFERENTIALS

In physics, you will often see equations involving physical quantities written as differentials. In order to give a discussion involving concepts which are generally familiar to you, we recall the first law of thermodynamics, which you have probably studied in your chemistry course. Suppose a system undergoes a change, in the course of which heat energy enters or leaves the system and the system either does work on its surroundings or work is done on the system by its surroundings. Then the first law of thermodynamics, which is really a statement of the conservation of energy, is usually expressed by the equation

$$\Delta U = Q - W \qquad (2.165)$$

In Eq. (2.165), Q is the energy added to the system by the transfer of heat, W is the energy given up by the system in doing work, and ΔU is the change in the internal energy of the system. Eq. (2.165) simply says that the change ΔU in the internal energy of the system is equal to the heat energy entering the system minus the energy leaving the system as work done by the system.

Now suppose that the process or change undergone by the system is a *very small* one, by which is meant that the physical variables involved change only by very small amounts. In this example, the physical variables involved are the internal energy U, the heat energy Q, and the energy W appearing as work, so the internal energy, heat, and work will change only by very small amounts. It is customary in physics to indicate "a very small amount of..." by using the notation for differentials. Thus,

dQ means "a very small amount of heat energy"
dW means "a very small amount of work (energy)"
dU means "a very small amount of internal energy."

Note that each of the symbols dQ, etc., is a single symbol (just like the symbol for the differential dx) and does *not* mean "d times Q." Using the symbols above, we may write the first law of thermodynamics for a

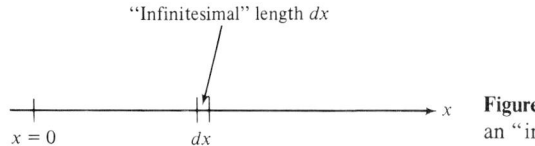

DERIVATIVES AND DIFFERENTIALS 53

"Infinitesimal" length dx

$x = 0$ dx $\longrightarrow x$ **Figure 2.6** The x axis, showing an "infinitesimal" length dx.

very small change undergone by the system as

$$dU = dQ - dW \qquad (2.166)$$

Eq. (2.166) is just the first law of thermodynamics stated for a very small change in a system. The equation says that the very small change dU in the internal energy is equal to the very small amount of energy dQ added to the system as heat minus the very small amount of work dW given up by the system in doing work.

The quantities dQ, etc., are also referred to as "infinitesimal quantities" or "differential quantities." Thus, dQ might be referred to as the infinitesimal quantity of heat energy, or the differential quantity of heat energy, entering the system. All of these terms for dQ, etc., signify the same physical meaning, namely, a very small amount of the quantity under discussion. Thus the symbol dA would in general mean "a very small amount of A," whatever physical quantity A may be.

Let's consider another example, this time from geometry, in Fig. 2.6, which shows the x axis. Suppose we consider a very short distance along the x axis, and give this very short length the symbol dx. Thus, dx means "a very small amount of distance along the x axis." It is customary to indicate such an "infinitesimal length" dx graphically as a short segment of the x axis, as shown in Fig. 2.6. This infinitesimal length dx might also be referred to as "an element of length" or the "differential distance" along the x axis.

We may discuss another example, this one involving the concept of *work*, which may already be familiar to you. If a force is applied to a body and moves it a distance in a direction parallel to the force, then the amount of work done is equal to the product of force times distance. Let's consider, as shown in Fig. 2.7, a force of constant magnitude F in a direction parallel to the x axis. Suppose that the force F moves a body a very small distance dx along the x axis. The amount of work done by the force on the body will be denoted by the

$x = 0$ dx $\longrightarrow F$ $\longrightarrow x$ **Figure 2.7** Force F parallel to the x axis.

symbol dW. Since work equals force times distance, we have

$$dW = F\,dx \qquad (2.167)$$

Eq. (2.167) says that the infinitesimal (i.e., very small) amount of work dW done on the body is equal to the product of the force F and the infinitesimal distance dx moved by the body. (Once again, keep in mind that both dW and dx are single symbols and are *not* the products of d with W or x.) Eq. (2.167) thus gives us the amount of work dW done in this infinitesimal process in which a force F moves a body an infinitesimal distance dx along the x axis. Note also that the force F is *not* considered infinitesimal in magnitude; only the distance dx and the amount of work dW are considered as very small.

We now have the idea of very small or infinitesimal amounts of physical quantities, such as heat or distance. These quantities, denoted by symbols dQ or dx, may be manipulated by the rules for the manipulation of differentials. In other words, these very small quantities dQ, etc., may be treated just like the mathematical differentials we discussed in the previous section.

Let's consider an example of the value of differentials of physical variables using Eq. (2.167) for the infinitesimal amount of work dW. Consider the very short time necessary for the body to move the infinitesimal distance dx under the influence of the constant force F. We will denote this very small amount of time by the symbol dt. We now consider the quantities dW, dx, and dt to be mathematical differentials and manipulate them accordingly. Specifically, we will divide both sides of Eq. (2.167) by the infinitesimal time dt, obtaining

$$\frac{dW}{dt} = \frac{F\,dx}{dt} = F\frac{dx}{dt} \qquad (2.168)$$

Eq. (2.168) says that the ratio (dW/dt) equals the force F times the ratio (dx/dt). Since we are treating dW, dx, and dt as differentials, the ratios (dW/dt) and (dx/dt) are derivatives and represent rates of change. The derivative (dW/dt) is the rate of change of work W done with respect to time t. The derivative (dx/dt) is the rate of change of distance x with respect to time t, so (dx/dt) is the velocity v. Substituting $v = (dx/dt)$ into Eq. (2.168) gives us

$$\frac{dW}{dt} = Fv \qquad (2.169)$$

an equation which says that the rate of change of work done with respect to time is equal to the product of the force times the velocity of the body. [We assume in Eq (2.169) that the force F and the velocity v are in the same direction.]

DERIVATIVES AND DIFFERENTIALS 55

Another important application of the differential is geometric, but is widely used in physics. This use is in differentials of the area or volume of a solid figure like a circle, sphere, cylinder, etc. Consider the area A of a circle of radius r, given by

$$A = \pi r^2 \qquad (2.170)$$

The differential dA of the area A of a circle is, on taking the differential of both sides of Eq. (2.170), given by

$$dA = 2\pi r \, dr \qquad (2.171)$$

where A is the dependent, and r the independent, variable.

Consider next, as shown in Fig. 2.8, a circular ring of width dr and radius r. We want to calculate the area dA of the circular ring. The area dA is just the difference between the area of a circle of radius $(r + dr)$ and the area of a circle of radius r. Thus

$$dA = \pi(r + dr)^2 - \pi r^2 = \pi r^2 + 2\pi r \, dr + \pi (dr)^2 - \pi r^2$$

$$dA = 2\pi r \, dr - \pi (dr)^2 \qquad (2.172)$$

In Eq. (2.172), we have the term $\pi(dr)^2$, which includes $(dr)^2$, the *square* of the differential dr. Since r is the radius of the ring, we interpret dr as a very small length, and the quantity $(dr)^2$ is the *square* of a very small quantity. We conclude that $(dr)^2$ is negligibly small compared to $2\pi r \, dr$ in Eq. (2.172). Indeed, we conclude that in general we are justified in neglecting a differential raised to any power higher than the first. With this proviso, we have from Eq. (2.172) that

$$dA = 2\pi r \, dr \qquad (2.173)$$

Eq. (2.173) says that the area dA of a circular ring of radius r and width dr is equal to $2\pi r \, dr$. Note that the area dA given by Eq. (2.173) is the same as the differential dA of the area of a circle given by Eq. (2.171).

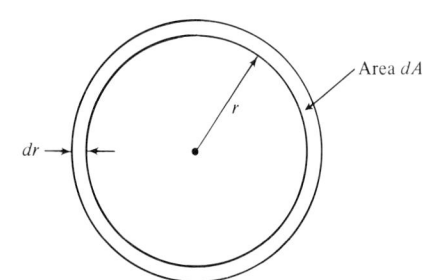

Figure 2.8 A circular ring of radius r and width dr. The area dA of the circular ring is equal to $2\pi r \, dr$.

56 CALCULUS FOR PHYSICS

The same kind of result holds true for the volume. Consider a sphere of radius r, whose volume V is given by

$$V = \frac{4\pi}{3} r^3 \tag{2.174}$$

The differential dV of the volume of a sphere is, from Eq. (2.174),

$$dV = 4\pi r^2 \, dr \tag{2.175}$$

We now calculate the volume dV of the thin spherical shell, of radius r and thickness dr, shown in Fig. 2.9. The volume dV of this spherical shell is

$$dV = \frac{4\pi}{3}(r + dr)^3 - \frac{4\pi}{3} r^3$$

$$dV = \frac{4\pi}{3}\left(r^3 + 3r^2 \, dr + 3r(dr)^2 + (dr)^3 - r^3\right) \tag{2.176}$$

Treating the terms containing $(dr)^2$ and $(dr)^3$ in Eq. (2.176) as negligible gives us

$$dV = 4\pi r^2 \, dr \tag{2.177}$$

for the volume of the spherical shell. Note again that this volume is equal to the differential dV of the volume of a sphere.

Differential elements of area and volume like Eq. (2.173) and Eq. (2.177) are widely used in setting up and solving physics problems involving geometric shapes. We will encounter them again when we discuss the applications of integrals to physics in Chapter 3.

As a final point on the physical interpretation of differentials, consider again the differential dy of a function $y = f(x)$, defined by the equation

$$dy = f'(x) \, dx \tag{2.178}$$

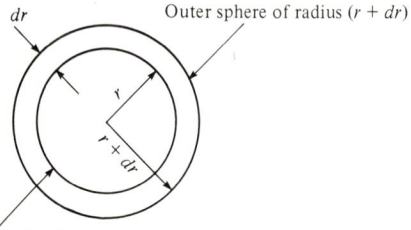

Figure 2.9 A spherical shell of radius r and thickness dr is the volume contained between two concentric spheres, one of radius $(r + dr)$ and one of radius r. The volume dV of the shell is $4\pi r^2 \, dr$.

DERIVATIVES AND DIFFERENTIALS 57

A common physical interpretation of Eq. (2.178) is as follows. Suppose the variable x changes by an infinitesimal amount dx. Then the corresponding change dy in y is given by Eq. (2.178) as the product of the derivative $f'(x)$ and dx. The basis for this interpretation lies in the fact that $f'(x)$ is the instantaneous rate of change of the function $f(x)$ with respect to x. That means that $f'(x)$ is the change in $f(x)$, or y, per unit of change in x, so $f'(x)$ times the change dx in x gives the total change dy in y. In physics, we generally consider the change dx to be very small, so the derivative $f'(x)$ can be considered as at least approximately constant in the interval of size dx over which x changes.

As an example, consider the function

$$y = f(x) = x^2$$

Suppose x changes from 1.00000 to 1.00001. What is the corresponding change in y? From Eq. (2.178),

$$dy = f'(x)\, dx = (2x)\, dx \qquad (2.179)$$

where the magnitude of the change dx in x is

$$dx = 0.00001$$

We now calculate the value of $f'(x) = 2x$. What value of x do we use? A reasonable choice is the value $x = 1.000005$, which lies halfway between the initial value $x = 1.00000$ and the final value $x = 1.00001$. We therefore take the value of $f'(x)$ in Eq. (2.179) as

$$f'(1.000005) = 2(1.000005) = 2.00001$$

Substituting this value of the derivative and the value $dx = 0.00001$ into Eq. (2.179) gives us

$$dy = (2.00001)(0.00001) \cong 0.00002 \qquad (2.180)$$

where the symbol "$\cong$" means "is approximately equal to." Eq. (2.180) says that the function $y = x^2$ changes by an amount $dy \cong 0.00002$ when x changes from the value 1.00000 to the value 1.00001.

This procedure of calculating (at least approximately) with Eq. (2.178) the change dy in a function $y = f(x)$, when the independent variable x changes by dx, is often encountered in physics and you will very probably see it used in your physics course.

This section illustrates how very small amounts of physical quantities (e.g., work) may be treated and manipulated as differentials. This approach is often used in physics and you will encounter it frequently. Further, this idea of using differentials in physics will come up again, and in a very important way, when we consider the applications of integral calculus.

Exercises

2.18 Consider a particle moving with a constant velocity v in a straight line on the x axis for a very short time dt. Using the familiar notion that rate times time equals distance, write the equation for the very short (infinitesimal) distance dx moved by the particle in the time dt.

2.19 Given the definition that acceleration a is the rate of change of velocity v with time t, as $a = (dv/dt)$. (a) Using this definition, calculate the differential dv of velocity in terms of a and dt. (b) Express in your own words the physical meaning of the equation you obtained as your result in (a).

2.20 Given the function $y = x^3$. Calculate the change in y when x changes from 2.00000 to 2.00001.

2.21 Consider a physical process in which a small quantity dQ of heat produces a small temperature increase dT in a mass m of a substance. It is found that dQ is directly proportional to the product $m\ dT$. (a) Using the symbol c for the constant of proportionality, write the equation giving dQ in terms of c, m, and dT. The quantity c, called the specific heat of the substance, is not really a constant, but is generally itself a function $c(T)$ of the temperature. (b) Consider the equation you found in (a), and divide both sides of it by the differential dT. Your result gives the specific heat in terms of (dQ/dT), the derivative of heat Q with respect to temperature T.

THE GEOMETRIC INTERPRETATION OF THE DERIVATIVE AND ITS PHYSICAL APPLICATIONS

While the most important interpretation of the derivative in physics is as a rate of change, we review here the geometric interpretation and discuss some of its applications. Given the function $f(x)$ of the variable x, consider the graph of $y = f(x)$ as a function of x shown in Fig. 2.10. We recall that, in discussing the definition of the derivative, we considered the ratio

$$\frac{f(x_1 + \Delta x) - f(x_1)}{\Delta x} \quad (2.181)$$

In Eq. (2.181), Δx is the increment in x, $f(x_1)$ is the value of the function f at the point $x = x_1$, and $f(x_1 + \Delta x)$ is the value of the function f at the point $x = (x_1 + \Delta x)$.

We now consider the meaning of the various quantities in Eq. (2.181) in terms of the graph of $y = f(x)$ in Fig. 2.10. The point A on the x axis is the point $x = x_1$; the point B is the point $x = (x_1 + \Delta x)$, so the distance **AB** (which equals the distance **CE**) along the x axis is equal to Δx. The distance **AC**, which equals the distance **BE**, is equal to the value $f(x_1)$ of the function $f(x)$ at the point x_1. Similarly, the distance **BD** is equal to the value $f(x_1 + \Delta x)$ of the function $f(x)$ at

DERIVATIVES AND DIFFERENTIALS

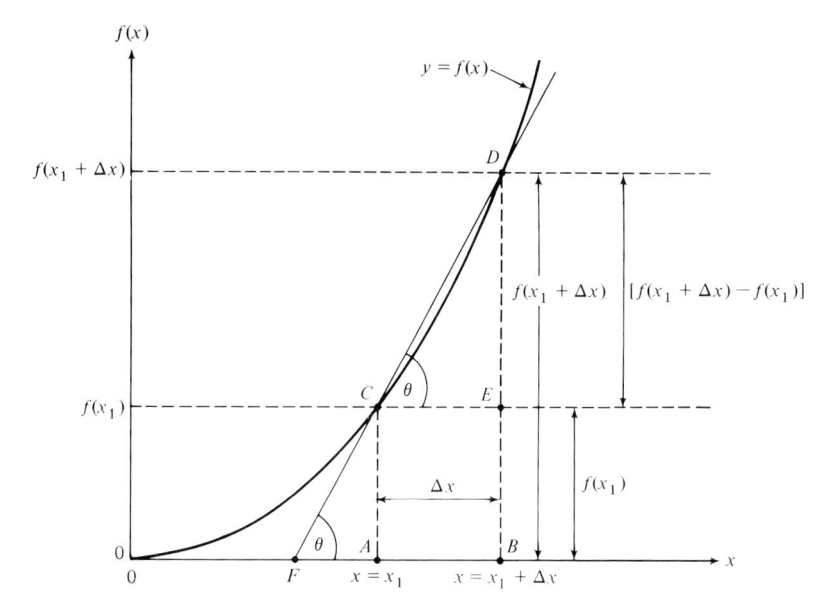

Figure 2.10 Graph of the function $f(x)$ as a function of x, showing the various quantities in Eq. (2.182).

the point $(x_1 + \Delta x)$. Finally, the distance **ED** is equal to the difference $[f(x_1 + \Delta x) - f(x_1)]$. Then, from Eq. (2.181), we have, since **AB** = **CE** = Δx, that

$$\frac{f(x_1 + \Delta x) - f(x_1)}{\Delta x} = \frac{ED}{CE} \qquad (2.182)$$

As shown in Fig. 2.10, we will denote the angle *DCE* by the symbol θ. Since line *CE* is parallel to the x axis, angle *DCE* equals angle *CFA*, and both are denoted by θ. From elementary trigonometry, the tangent of the angle *DCE* is equal to the ratio of the length *ED* to the length *CE*. Thus it is true, from Eq. (2.182), that

$$\frac{f(x_1 + \Delta x) - f(x_1)}{\Delta x} = \tan \theta \qquad (2.183)$$

where, as shown in Fig. 2.10, θ is the angle the straight line *DCF* makes with the x axis. By the definition of the *slope* of a straight line given in Chapter 1, Eq. (2.183) gives us the important result that the quantity

$$\frac{f(x_1 + \Delta x) - f(x_1)}{\Delta x} \qquad (2.184)$$

is equal to the *slope* of the straight line DCF passing through the point C (at the point $x = x_1$) on the graph of the function $f(x)$.

Let us now take the limit, as the quantity Δx becomes smaller, of the quantity in expression (2.184). We can see what happens on the graph in Fig. 2.10 as Δx decreases. As Δx becomes smaller, the point D moves to the left along the curve $f(x)$ and approaches the point C. Eventually, as Δx becomes very small, the line DCF approaches (and becomes) the geometric tangent to the curve $f(x)$ at the point C where $x = x_1$. (Do not confuse the geometric tangent with the mathematical function $\tan \theta$.) Mathematically, we indicate the process of Δx becoming very small by writing $\Delta x \to 0$, and indicate the effect on the quantity in Eq. (2.184) by writing

$$\lim_{\Delta x \to 0} \frac{f(x_1 + \Delta x) - f(x_1)}{\Delta x} \qquad (2.185)$$

We therefore conclude that, as $\Delta x \to 0$, the line DCF becomes the geometric tangent to the curve $f(x)$ at the point $x = x_1$. From Eq. (2.183), we conclude also that the value of the limit approached in Eq. (2.185) is equal to the value of the tangent of the angle θ, where θ is the angle made by the geometric tangent with the x axis.

Next, we see that the limit expression in Eq. (2.185) defines the derivative $f'(x_1)$, of $f(x)$ with respect to x, at the point $x = x_1$. We thus conclude that

$$\lim_{\Delta x \to 0} \frac{f(x_1 + \Delta x) - f(x_1)}{\Delta x} = f'(x_1) = \tan \theta \qquad (2.186)$$

where θ is the angle made with the x axis by the geometric tangent to the curve of $f(x)$ at the point $x = x_1$. Since the quantity $\tan \theta$ in Eq. (2.186) is the slope of the geometric tangent, that equation says that

$$f'(x_1) = \tan \theta = \text{slope of geometric tangent at point } x = x_1$$

$$(2.187)$$

Eq. (2.187) says that the derivative $f'(x_1)$, at the point $x = x_1$, gives the slope of the geometric tangent to the curve at the point $x = x_1$. Fig. 2.11 shows the graph of Fig. 2.10 redrawn to show the geometric tangent at the point C where $x = x_1$. The geometric tangent makes an angle θ with the x axis and the value of the angle θ is given by Eq. (2.187), meaning that a knowledge of the value of the derivative $f'(x_1)$ at the point $x = x_1$ gives us the value of $\tan \theta$, the tangent of the angle θ, which we can use to find the angle θ itself.

DERIVATIVES AND DIFFERENTIALS **61**

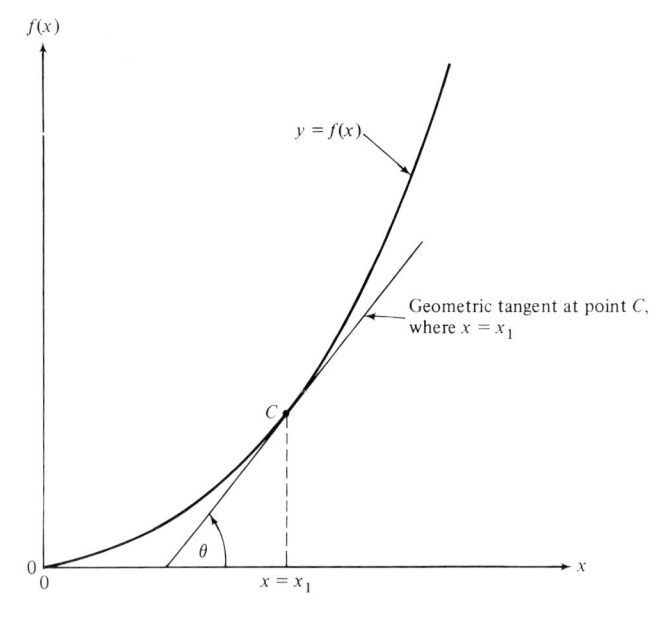

Figure 2.11 Graph of the function $f(x)$ as a function of x, showing the geometric tangent to the curve at the point C at which $x = x_1$. The slope $\tan \theta$ of the geometric tangent is equal to $f'(x_1)$, the value of the derivative at $x = x_1$.

Let's consider a specific example of these ideas. Consider the function

$$y = f(x) = \tfrac{1}{4}x^2 + 1$$

whose derivative is

$$\frac{dy}{dx} = f'(x) = \frac{x}{2} \qquad (2.188)$$

The graph of the function $y = f(x) = (1/4)x^2 + 1$ is shown in Fig. 2.12. Let's find the slope of the geometric tangent to the curve at the point C at which $x = 2$. From Eq. (2.188), the value of the derivative at $x = 2$ is

$$\left(\frac{dy}{dx}\right)_{x=2} = f'(2) = \frac{2}{2} = 1$$

so, from Eq. (2.187), we have

$$\tan \theta = 1 \qquad (2.189)$$

where $\tan \theta$ is (by definition) the slope of the geometric tangent, so

62 CALCULUS FOR PHYSICS

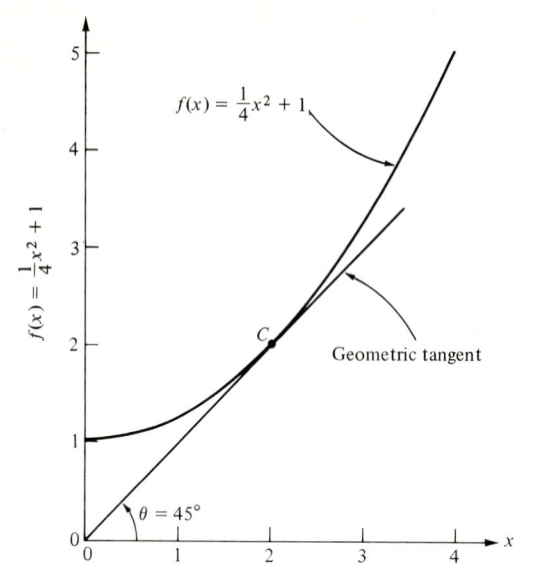

Figure 2.12 Graph of the function $y = (x^2/4) + 1$, showing the geometric tangent at the point $x = 2$. The slope of the geometric tangent has the value $\tan \theta = 1$, so the angle $\theta = 45°$. In this example, the geometric tangent happens to pass through the origin.

that the slope is equal to 1. To find the angle θ itself, we solve Eq. (2.189) for θ, obtaining

$$\theta = \tan^{-1} 1 = 45°$$

so the geometric tangent makes an angle of 45° with the x axis, as shown in Fig. 2.12.

Finally, we should note the following point of terminology. The slope $f'(x_1)$ of the geometric tangent to the curve $f(x)$ at $x = x_1$ is (by definition) called the *slope of the curve* $f(x)$ at the point $x = x_1$. In other words, the slope of the geometric tangent at a point is the slope of the curve itself at that point. In the future, we will use the term "slope of the curve" synonomously with "slope of the geometric tangent."

One of the most important uses in physics of the geometric interpretation of the derivative is in discussing graphs of position, velocity, and acceleration as functions of time. Suppose we return to Eq. (2.129),

$$s = f(t) = 4.9t^2 \tag{2.129}$$

which gives the distance s moved by a body falling vertically from rest

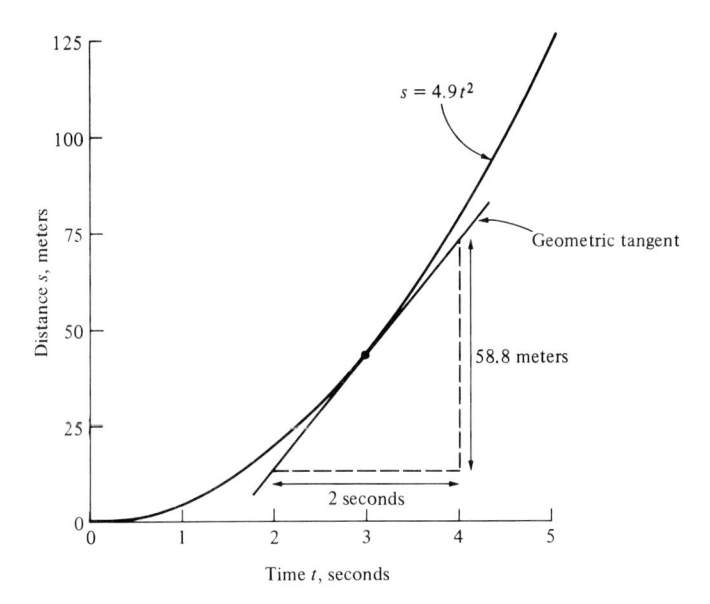

Figure 2.13 Graph of $s = 4.9t^2$ as a function of t, where s is the distance in meters and t is the time in seconds. Also shown is the geometric tangent (of slope 29.4 meters per second) at a point $t = 3$ seconds.

(without air resistance) as a function of time t. In Eq. (2.129), s is in meters and t is in seconds. Fig. 2.13 shows a graph of s as a function of t from Eq. (2.129) for times from $t = 0$ to $t = 5$ seconds; the graph is a parabola passing through the origin.

The derivative of s with respect to t is given by

$$\frac{ds}{dt} = f'(t) = 9.8t \qquad (2.190)$$

and, since the velocity v is the rate of change of distance with respect to time, $v = (ds/dt) = f'(t)$, so we have

$$v = 9.8t \qquad (2.191)$$

Eq. (2.190) for $f'(t)$ gives the slope of the curve $s = f(t) = 4.9t^2$. Eq. (2.191) gives the velocity as a function of time. Comparison of Eqs. (2.190) and (2.191) gives us the following useful result. The slope of the graph of distance as a function of time is the velocity. Thus if we calculate the slope of the curve of distance (as a function of time) at some value of the time, we have also calculated the value of the velocity at that value of the time.

64 CALCULUS FOR PHYSICS

As an example, consider the slope of the curve $s = 4.9t^2$ at the point $t = 3$ seconds. From Eq. (2.190), the slope is given by

$$\left(\frac{ds}{dt}\right)_{t=3} = f'(3) = (9.8)(3) = 29.4$$

which, from Eq. (2.191), is equal to the velocity, so

$$v = 29.4 \text{ meters per second}$$

at the instant of time $t = 3$ seconds. Fig. 2.13 also shows the geometric tangent, of slope 29.4 meters per second, at the point $t = 3$ seconds. Note that, since the velocity is equal to the slope, the slope of the graph of distance (meters) as a function of time (seconds) is expressed in meters per second.

Using Eq. (2.191), we can also make a graph of the velocity v as a function of time. This is shown in Fig. 2.14, and is the graph of the equation $v = 9.8t$ for values of t from 0 to 5 seconds. As seen from the graph, the velocity increases linearly with increasing time, and we can find the velocity at any instant of time from the graph. For instance, when the time $t = 2$ seconds, $v = 19.6$ meters per second. Note that Fig. 2.14 is really a graph of the derivative $f'(t)$, given by Eq. (2.190), as a function of time. Thus Fig. 2.14 is a graph of the slope of the curve $s = 4.9t^2$, plotted as a function of time.

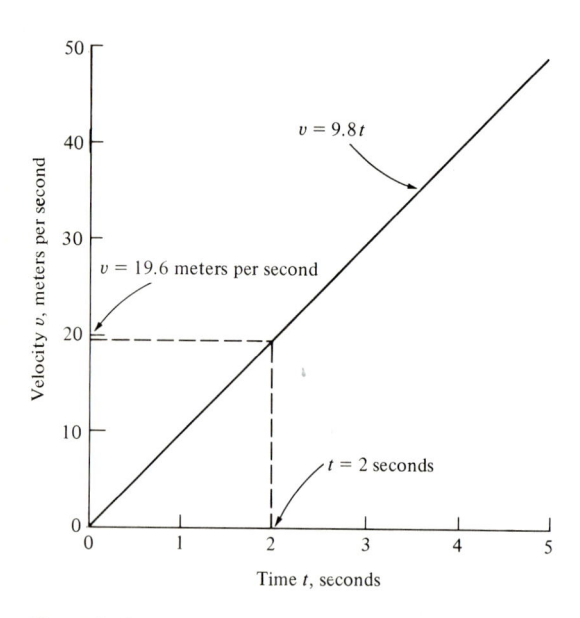

Figure 2.14 Graph of $v = 9.8t$ as a function of t, where v is the velocity in meters per second and t is the time in seconds.

Last, we may consider the slope of the "curve" (which is a straight line) in Fig. 2.14. Since Fig. 2.14 is a graph of velocity as a function of time, the slope of the curve is given by

$$\frac{dv}{dt} = f''(t) = 9.8 \qquad (2.192)$$

on differentiating Eq. (2.191) with respect to time. Eq. (2.192) says that the slope of the straight line graph in Fig. 2.14 has the constant value 9.8, expressed in (meters per second) per second. Since the derivative (dv/dt) is the rate of change of velocity with respect to time, Eq. (2.192) gives us the acceleration a, where

$$a = 9.8 \text{ (meters per second) per second} \qquad (2.193)$$

From this example, we see the following important result. The slope of the graph of velocity as a function of time is the acceleration. In this example, the acceleration is constant and does not vary with time. This is shown in Fig. 2.15, which is a graph of the acceleration a given by Eq. (2.193). Since a is constant, its graph as a function of time is horizontal because it does not change with time. Note also that the result contained in Eq. (2.192) agrees with the result from analytical geometry that the slope of a straight line is constant.

We may conclude this section by summarizing some of our important conclusions about the geometric interpretation of the derivative. Given the graph of the function $f(x)$ as a function of x, the

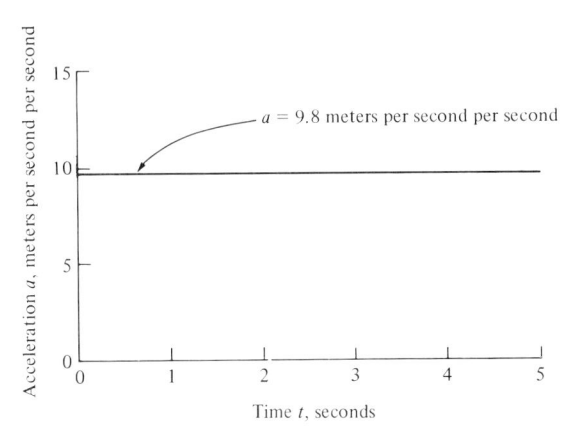

Figure 2.15 Graph of $a = 9.8$ as a function of time t, where a is the acceleration in (meters per second) per second. The acceleration is constant in this example and does not vary with time.

derivative $f'(x)$ gives the slope of the curve. The value $f'(x_1)$ of the derivative at the point $x = x_1$ gives the slope of the curve at that point. The slope (ds/dt) of a graph of distance s as a function of time t is equal to the velocity v. The slope (dv/dt) of a graph of velocity v as a function of time t is equal to the acceleration a.

Exercises

2.22 (a) Calculate the slope of the geometric tangent to the curve $y = x^2 + 2$ at the point $x = 5$; (b) What angle θ does the geometric tangent make with the x axis? (c) Calculate the slope of the curve at the point $x = 2$.

2.23 In a certain physics experiment, the distance s a body moves (from rest) as a function of time is given by

$$s = 2t^3$$

where s is in meters and t is in seconds. (a) Make a graph of s as a function of t for values of t from 0 to 2 seconds at intervals of 0.1 second. (b) Calculate the slope of the curve in (a) at $t = 1$ second; (c) Calculate the velocity v of the body, and make a graph of v as a function of t for the same time interval used in (a). What is the name of this curve?; (d) Calculate the slope of the curve in (c) at $t = 1$ second; (e) Calculate the acceleration a of the body, and make a graph of a as a function of t for the same time interval used in (a) and (c). What is the name of this curve?; (f) Is the acceleration constant? Give your reasons.

MAXIMA AND MINIMA

We conclude our discussion of the applications of derivatives to physics by considering problems involving maxima and minima of functions. We will assume that all of the functions we encounter in elementary physics are well-behaved in that their derivatives exist, are not infinite, etc. Discussion of such unusual cases will be found in calculus textbooks.

We review the key results on maxima and minima, which it is assumed you have seen in your calculus course. Given a function $f(x)$, f is said to have a relative *maximum* at the point $x = a$ if

$$f(a) \geq f(a + \varepsilon) \tag{2.194}$$

for all small (i.e., near zero) positive and negative values of ε. Eq. (2.194) says that the function $f(x)$ has a greater value at the point $x = a$ than it does at the neighboring points $x = a \pm \varepsilon$. Similarly, $f(x)$ is said to have a relative *minimum* at the point $x = b$ if

$$f(b) \leq f(b + \varepsilon) \tag{2.195}$$

DERIVATIVES AND DIFFERENTIALS **67**

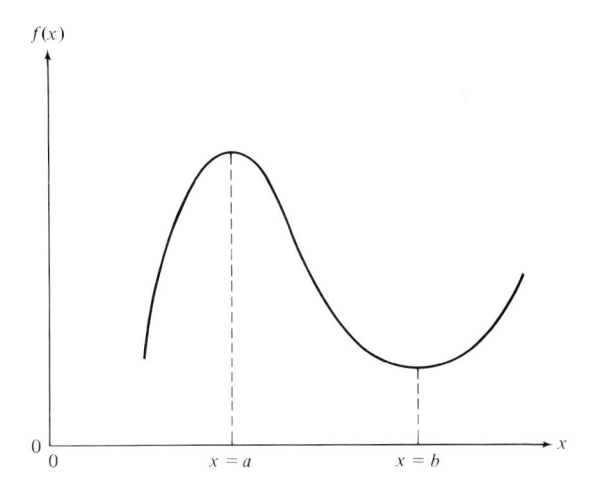

Figure 2.16 Graph of the function $f(x)$ showing a relative maximum at $x = a$ and a relative minimum at $x = b$.

an equation which says $f(x)$ has a smaller value at the point $x = b$ than it does at the neighboring points $x = b \pm \epsilon$. Fig. 2.16 shows a relative maximum at $x = a$, and a relative minimum at $x = b$, for the function $f(x)$. The graph is said to be concave downward around $x = a$ and concave upward around $x = b$.

If the function $f(x)$ has a relative maximum or minimum at the point $x = c$, then it is true that

$$f'(c) = 0 \qquad (2.196)$$

Equation (2.196) says that the derivative $f'(x)$ vanishes at a point $x = c$ at which there is a relative maximum or a relative minimum. A point such as $x = c$ is called a *critical* point. In Fig. 2.16, $x = a$ and $x = b$ are critical points and it is therefore true that both $f'(a) = 0$ and $f'(b) = 0$. The derivative vanishes at the point $x = a$ where the function has a maximum and at the point $x = b$ where there is a minimum.

The second derivative gives us information on whether we are dealing with a maximum or a minimum. If, at $x = c$, $f'(c) = 0$ and $f''(c)$ is positive, then the function $f(x)$ has a minimum at $x = c$. If $f'(c) = 0$ and $f''(c)$ is negative, then $f(x)$ has a maximum at $x = c$. (If $f'(c) = 0$ and $f''(c) = 0$, then the test fails and gives no information.) Referring to the curve in Fig. 2.16, $f''(a)$ would be negative since there is a maximum at $x = a$ and $f''(b)$ would be positive since there is a minimum at $x = b$.

As an example, consider the function

$$y = f(x) = 6x - x^2 \qquad (2.197)$$

a downwardly concave parabola whose axis is parallel to the y axis. To find a critical point, we calculate the derivative $f'(x)$ and set it equal to zero, so we have

$$f'(x) = 6 - 2x = 0 \qquad (2.198)$$

We solve Eq. (2.198) and find $x = 3$, so $f'(3) = 0$. Since the derivative equals zero at $x = 3$, there is either a maximum or a minimum at that point. To find out which, we examine the second derivative, which is

$$f''(x) = -2 \qquad (2.199)$$

Since $f''(x)$ at $x = 3$ is negative (it has the value -2 for all values of x), there is a maximum at $x = 3$. Finally, we may calculate the value of the function $f(x)$ at this maximum by finding $f(3)$, the value of the function at the critical point $x = 3$. From Eq. (2.197), $f(3) = 9$, so the function $f(x)$ has the value 9 at this maximum. The graph of the function $f(x) = 6x - x^2$ as shown in Fig. 2.17.

It is often useful in physics to find the maximum or minimum of some function. As an example, let's consider a stone thrown vertically upward with an initial velocity of 9.8 meters per second. By "initial," we mean the velocity at the instant of time $t = 0$ when the upward motion begins. If, as usual, air resistance is neglected, the height y of

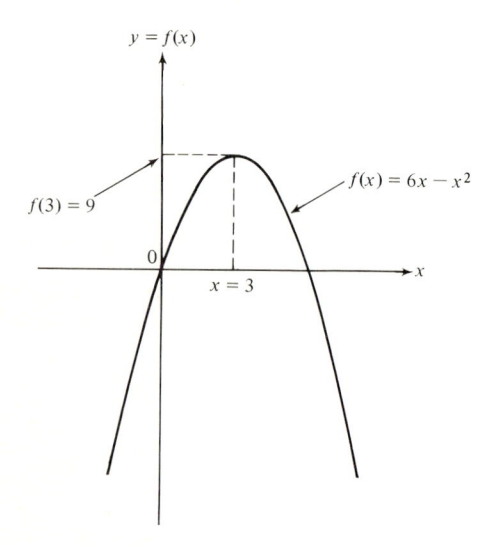

Figure 2.17 Graph of the function $y = f(x) = 6x - x^2$, showing the maximum at $x = 3$.

the stone as a function of time t is found to be

$$y = f(t) = 9.8t - 4.9t^2 \qquad (2.200)$$

Eq. (2.200) gives the vertical height y, measured from zero height ($y = 0$) at the start of the motion when $t = 0$, as a function $f(t)$ of time. We ask two questions. First, how long does it take the stone to reach its maximum height? Second, what is the maximum height?

We answer the first question by calculating the value of the time t at which the height y is a maximum. (We know y will have a maximum, and not a minimum, value based on our physical knowledge of the situation.) To find this value of t, we find the derivative (dy/dt) and set it equal to zero, obtaining

$$\frac{dy}{dt} = f'(t) = 9.8 - 9.8t = 0 \qquad (2.201)$$

We solve this equation for t, obtaining $t = 1$ second as the value of the time at which y is a maximum. Thus it takes the stone 1 second to reach its maximum height. We may check that we are dealing with a maximum in y by noting from Eq. (2.201) that the second derivative (d^2y/dt^2) = -9.8 (meters per second per second) and thus is negative.

We answer the second question by finding the maximum value of y, i.e., the value of y when $t = 1$ second. We denote the maximum value of y by the symbol y_{max}, where, from Eq. (2.200),

$$y_{max} = f(1) = 9.8(1) - 4.9(1)^2 = 4.9 \text{ meters} \qquad (2.202)$$

The maximum height, y_{max}, to which the stone rises is 4.9 meters.

As a final point about this example, we note that the derivative (dy/dt) is the rate of change of vertical height with respect to time. The derivative (dy/dt) is thus the velocity v_y of the stone in the vertical direction, so we have

$$v_y = \frac{dy}{dt} = 9.8 - 9.8t \qquad (2.203)$$

on differentiating Eq. (2.200) with respect to time. Eq. (2.203) gives us the vertical velocity v_y at any time t. We note that the requirement (dy/dt) = 0 that the height have its maximum value is identical to the statement that the vertical velocity $v_y = 0$. The vertical velocity is zero at the instant when the height is a maximum, a conclusion that is true in general. In this example, the vertical velocity is zero at the instant ($t = 1$ second) at which the height has its maximum value of 4.9 meters.

Exercises

2.24 Given the function $f(x) = \sin x$. Considering only positive values of x, find (a) the value of x at which $f(x)$ has its first maximum; (b) the value of x at which $f(x)$ has its first minimum; (c) apply the second derivative test to parts (a) and (b).

2.25 You will find in your physics course the following physical problem. Suppose a ball is thrown from the origin $(0, 0)$ with initial velocity v_0 at time $t = 0$. Suppose further that the direction in which it is thrown makes an initial angle θ with the horizontal direction. Then, if the x axis is the horizontal direction and the y axis is the vertical direction, the coordinates (x, y) of the ball are given as functions of time t by the equations

$$x = (v_0 \cos \theta) t$$

$$y = (v_0 \sin \theta) t - 4.9 t^2$$

where x and y are in meters, t is in seconds, and v_0 is in meters per second. (a) Calculate the value of the time at which the vertical height is a maximum; (b) Calculate the value of the horizontal distance traveled when the vertical height is a maximum. (Your answers to both parts will be in terms of v_0 and θ.)

CHAPTER
THREE
SUMS AND INTEGRALS

INTRODUCTION

In this chapter, we treat some of the applications of integral calculus to problems in physics. After a review of the integral as an antiderivative and of some techniques for evaluating integrals, the relation between constants of integration and initial conditions in physics problems is discussed. Next, the definition and evaluation of definite integrals are reviewed. The geometric interpretation of the definite integral precedes a discussion of its interpretation as a "sum of infinitesimal elements." Last, some physical applications of the definite integral are presented, using examples from several areas of physics, and emphasizing the use of the integral as a sum.

REVIEW OF INTEGRALS AS ANTIDERIVATIVES

Suppose we have two functions, $F(x)$ and $f(x)$, of the independent variable x, such that the derivative of $F(x)$ is equal to $f(x)$, so

$$\frac{dF(x)}{dx} = f(x) \qquad (3.1)$$

72 CALCULUS FOR PHYSICS

If we multiply both sides of Eq. (3.1) by the differential dx, we obtain

$$dF(x) = f(x)\,dx \qquad (3.2)$$

an equation which says that the differential $dF(x)$, of the function $F(x)$, is equal to the function $f(x)$ times dx.

Suppose further that we know $f(x)$ and want to find $F(x)$. In other words, as seen from Eq. (3.1), we know the *derivative* of $F(x)$ and we want to find the function $F(x)$ itself. We may say the same thing, with reference to Eq. (3.2), by saying that, since we know $f(x)$, we know the *differential* $dF(x)$ and we want to find $F(x)$. The process of finding the function $F(x)$ when we know its derivative $(dF/dx) = f(x)$, and/or its differential $dF = f(x)\,dx$, is called *integration* or finding the *antiderivative*. When we differentiate a function, we go from the function to its derivative and differential. When we integrate, we go from the derivative and differential of the function to the function itself. Integration is thus the *inverse* of differentiation. Thus $f(x)$ is the derivative of $F(x)$ and $F(x)$ is the antiderivative or integral of $f(x)$. We indicate that $F(x)$ is the integral or antiderivative of $f(x)$ by writing

$$F(x) = \int f(x)\,dx \qquad (3.3)$$

where the symbol $\int$ is called the integral sign and the function $f(x)$ under the integral sign is called the *integrand*. Eq. (3.3) is read "$F(x)$ is the integral of $f(x)\,dx$" and means that $F(x)$ is the antiderivative of $f(x)$ since $f(x)$ is the derivative of $F(x)$.

Let's consider an example. Suppose the derivative of a function $F(x)$ is $2x$, so

$$\frac{dF(x)}{dx} = 2x \qquad (3.4)$$

and, in terms of differentials,

$$dF(x) = 2x\,dx \qquad (3.5)$$

so the function $f(x)$ is $2x$. We know that x^2 is the function whose derivative is $2x$, so we have

$$F(x) = x^2 \qquad (3.6)$$

We can see that Eqs. (3.4) and (3.6) are consistent because differentiating both sides of (3.6) gives (3.4). We say that we have *integrated* the function $2x$ to obtain its antiderivative x^2. In the notation of Eq. (3.3),

$$x^2 = \int 2x\, dx \tag{3.7}$$

an equation which says that the antiderivative or integral of $2x$ is x^2. In the notation of Eq. (3.5),

$$d(x^2) = 2x\, dx \tag{3.8}$$

an equation the says that differential of x^2 is $(2x)\, dx$.

To recapitulate, the process of finding the function $F(x)$ when we know its derivative $f(x)$, or its differential $f(x)\, dx$, is called integration or antidifferentiation. Integration thus constitutes the process that is the *inverse* of differentiation.

In Eq. (3.6), we found the function $F(x) = x^2$ whose derivative is $f(x) = 2x$, and we saw that the derivative of Eq. (3.6) was Eq. (3.4). Suppose we add a constant C to the right-hand side of Eq. (3.6), which then becomes

$$F(x) = x^2 + C \tag{3.9}$$

If we differentiate both sides of Eq. (3.9), we obtain

$$\frac{dF(x)}{dx} = 2x \tag{3.10}$$

because the derivative of any constant is zero. From Eqs. (3.9) and (3.10), we see that not only is the function x^2 the antiderivative of $2x$, but the function $(x^2 + C)$, where C is *any* constant, is also the antiderivative of $2x$. The constant C is called a *constant of integration*. We thus rewrite Eq. (3.3) to read

$$F(x) + C = \int f(x)\, dx \tag{3.11}$$

which says that the integral (or antiderivative) of $f(x)$ is the function $F(x)$ plus the constant of integration C. The fact that C can be any constant is sometimes stated by saying that C is an arbitrary constant. Integrals containing a constant of integration, like the one in Eq. (3.11), are called *indefinite* integrals; the reason for this name will become clear later.

You will often see Eq. (3.11) written in the form

$$F(x) + C = \int dF(x) \tag{3.12}$$

where we have used the fact, contained in Eq. (3.2),

$$dF(x) = f(x)\, dx \qquad (3.2)$$

that the differential $dF(x)$ of $F(x)$ is equal to $f(x)\,dx$. The content of Eq. (3.12) may be stated by saying that the integral of the differential $dF(x)$ is the function $F(x)$ plus the constant C. Thus, in Eq. (3.7), x^2 is the integral of the differential $d(x^2) = 2x\,dx$, so we write

$$x^2 + C = \int d(x^2) = \int 2x\, dx \qquad (3.13)$$

Note that Eq. (3.13) is just a combination of Eqs. (3.7) and (3.8). We may combine Eqs. (3.12) and (3.2) to give

$$F(x) + C = \int dF(x) = \int f(x)\, dx \qquad (3.14)$$

In integrals such as those in Eq. (3.14), we call x "the variable of integration" or say we are "integrating over the variable x."

Let's consider another example. Suppose

$$\frac{dF(x)}{dx} = f(x) = e^x \qquad (3.15)$$

where e^x is the exponential function. We know from Eq. (2.37) that e^x is the function whose derivative is e^x. Thus, the antiderivative $F(x) = e^x$, and we have

$$e^x + C = \int e^x\, dx \qquad (3.16)$$

where C is the arbitrary constant of integration. We can test our antiderivative in Eq. (3.16) by noting that the derivative of the left-hand side of Eq. (3.16) does indeed equal e^x, the function whose integral we are seeking.

If $u(x)$ and $v(x)$ are functions of x, and a and n are constants ($n \neq 1$), then the following are some properties of integrals:

$$\int (u + v)\, dx = \int u\, dx + \int v\, dx \qquad (3.17)$$

$$\int au\, dx = a \int u\, dx \qquad (3.18)$$

Thus, as an example,

$$2 \int x\, dx = \int (2x)\, dx = x^2 + C \qquad (3.19)$$

The following are some simple integrals which are frequently encountered in physics.

$$\int dx = x + C \qquad (3.20)$$

$$\int x^n \, dx = \frac{x^{n+1}}{n+1} + C \qquad (n \neq -1) \qquad (3.21)$$

$$\int e^x \, dx = e^x + C \qquad (3.22)$$

$$\int \sin x \, dx = -\cos x + C \qquad (3.23)$$

$$\int \cos x \, dx = \sin x + C \qquad (3.24)$$

As an example of the integration formulas above, consider Eq. (3.21) with $n = 3$. We have

$$\int x^3 \, dx = (x^4/4) + C \qquad (3.25)$$

we can see that Eq. (3.25) is correct because x^3 is indeed the derivative of $(x^4/4)$.

How does one find the integral of a function that is more complicated than the simple functions above? There are a variety of techniques of integration which are covered in your calculus book. There are, however, two which are often encountered in physics and which we will discuss here.

The first of these is integration by *substitution*. In this technique, best described by example, a substitution changes a complicated integral into a simpler one which is readily evaluated. As a first example, consider the integral

$$\int e^{ax} \, dx \qquad (3.26)$$

where a is a constant. Suppose we make the substitution

$$ax = u \qquad (3.27)$$

then the differential dx is related to the differential du of the new variable u by

$$a \, dx = du \qquad (3.28)$$

$$dx = (1/a) \, du \qquad (3.29)$$

Substituting Eqs. (3.29) and (3.27) into Eq. (3.26) reduces the integral

76 CALCULUS FOR PHYSICS

in Eq. (3.26) to

$$\int e^{ax} dx = \int e^u \left(\frac{1}{a}\right) du = \frac{1}{a} \int e^u du = \frac{1}{a} e^u + C \qquad (3.30)$$

Then, since $u = ax$, Eq. (3.30) becomes the desired result

$$\int e^{ax} dx = \frac{1}{a} e^{ax} + C \qquad (3.31)$$

We can check the correctness of Eq. (3.31) by noting that the derivative of $(1/a)e^{ax}$ is e^{ax}. (Under the heading of notation, it is worth pointing out that the exponential function is often written exp x. Thus

$$\exp x \equiv e^x \qquad (3.32)$$

a form you will encounter frequently.)

As a second example, consider the integral

$$\int x(2x^2 - 1)^{1/2} dx \qquad (3.33)$$

Let's make the substitution

$$u = 2x^2 - 1 \qquad (3.34)$$

$$du = 4x \, dx \qquad (3.35)$$

so

$$(1/4) \, du = x \, dx \qquad (3.36)$$

Substituting Eqs. (3.36) and (3.34) into the integral in Eq. (3.33) gives

$$\int x(2x^2 - 1)^{1/2} dx = \int u^{1/2} \frac{du}{4} = \left(\frac{1}{4}\right) \int u^{1/2} du = \left(\frac{1}{4}\right)\left(\frac{2}{3}\right) u^{3/2} + C \qquad (3.37)$$

Since $u = (2x^2 - 1)$, our final result is

$$\int x(2x^2 - 1)^{1/2} dx = (1/6)(2x^2 - 1)^{3/2} + C \qquad (3.38)$$

Keep in mind that choosing a useful substitution is at least partly based on experience, so practice is very helpful in evaluating integrals.

The second technique of integration we will discuss is called integration *by parts*. This method is based on the differential of the product of two functions $u(x)$ and $v(x)$. Then the differential of the product is, from Eq. (2.164),

$$d(uv) = u \, dv + v \, du \qquad (3.39)$$

so

$$u \, dv = d(uv) - v \, du \qquad (3.40)$$

If we integrate both sides of Eq. (3.40), we get

$$\int u\, dv = \int d(uv) - \int v\, du \qquad (3.41)$$

From Eq. (3.12), the integral of the differential of a function is the function itself, so

$$\int d(uv) = uv \qquad (3.42)$$

Using Eq. (3.42), Eq. (3.41) becomes

$$\int u\, dv = uv - \int v\, du \qquad (3.43)$$

Eq. (3.43) expresses the integral $\int u\, dv$ in terms of a second integral $\int v\, du$, and the product uv. Often a wise choice (again usually based on experience) of u and v will make the second integral simpler than the first, so Eq. (3.43) may be used to evaluate $\int u\, dv$.

A standard example illustrating integration by parts is the evaluation of

$$\int \ln x\, dx \qquad (3.44)$$

Choose

$$u = \ln x \qquad (3.45)$$
$$du = (1/x)\, dx \qquad (3.46)$$
$$dv = dx \qquad (3.47)$$

so

$$v = \int dv = \int dx = x + C_1 \qquad (3.48)$$

where C_1 is a constant of integration. Then

$$uv = (x + C_1)\ln x = x\ln x + C_1 \ln x \qquad (3.49)$$

and, applying Eq. (3.43), we obtain

$$\int \ln x\, dx = [x\ln x + C_1 \ln x] - \int (x + C_1)(1/x)\, dx \qquad (3.50)$$

$$\int \ln x\, dx = [x\ln x + C_1 \ln x] - \int dx - \int \frac{C_1}{x}\, dx + C_2 \qquad (3.51)$$

where C_2 is another constant of integration. Then, since

$$\int (1/x)\, dx = \ln x \qquad (3.52)$$

Eq. (3.51) becomes

$$\int \ln x \, dx = x \ln x + C_1 \ln x - x - C_1 \ln x + C_2 \quad (3.53)$$

so

$$\int \ln x \, dx = x \ln x - x + C_2 = x(\ln x - 1) + C_2 \quad (3.54)$$

gives us the required answer. (Note that the constant C_1 does not appear in the final answer.)

Last, it should be mentioned here that there are a number of collections of tables of integrals available. These contain many integrals; such a table is doubtless included in your calculus text. There are also books which are tables of integrals. A useful one is *Tables of Integrals and Other Mathematical Data* by H. B. Dwight,* which contains several hundred integrals in addition to trigonometric and algebraic material. From now on, it will be assumed that the reader is able to evaluate the integrals we encounter.

Exercises

3.1 Evaluate the following integral by substitution: $\int \cos 3x \, dx$.
3.2 Evaluate the following integral by substitution: $\int (x - a)^2 \, dx$, where a is a constant.
3.3 Evaluate the following integral by substitution: $\int x \, e^{-x^2} \, dx$.
3.4 Evaluate the following integral by parts: $\int x \cos x \, dx$.
3.5 Evaluate the following integral by parts: $\int x \, e^x \, dx$.

CONSTANTS OF INTEGRATION AND INITIAL CONDITIONS

Let's consider next the application of integration to a physical problem. Suppose a particle moves in one direction along a straight line, and suppose also that its acceleration a has a constant magnitude equal to A. Written as an equation, this statement is

$$a = \frac{dv}{dt} = A \quad (3.55)$$

In Eq. (3.55), we also put in the fact that the acceleration a is equal to (dv/dt), the rate of change of velocity v with respect to time. Our aim is to use Eq. (3.55) to find the velocity as a function $v(t)$ of the time t.

---

*H. B. Dwight, *Tables of Integrals and Other Mathematical Data*, 4th ed., Macmillan, New York, 1961.

Starting with

$$\frac{dv}{dt} = A \qquad (3.56)$$

we multiply both sides of Eq. (3.56) by dt, the differential of the time t, obtaining

$$dv = A\,dt \qquad (3.57)$$

Eq. (3.57) gives the differential dv of the velocity v as equal to the constant A times dt, so this equation gives us the differential dv of the function $v(t)$ we are seeking. Since we know dv, we can find $v(t)$ by integrating Eq. (3.57). The result is

$$v(t) = \int dv = \int A\,dt \qquad (3.58)$$

where we write the velocity as $v(t)$ to emphasize that v is a function of the time; the variable of integration in Eq. (3.58) is the time t. Since A is a constant, Eq. (3.58) becomes

$$v(t) + C' = A\int dt \qquad (3.59)$$

where C' is a constant of integration, and so our result is

$$v(t) + C' = At \qquad (3.60)$$

In Eq. (3.60), we put the constant C' on the left-hand side of the equation, thus writing Eq. (3.61) in the same form as that used in Eq. (3.14). Note, however, that we could have equally well put a constant C on the right-hand side of the equation, in which case Eq. (3.60) becomes

$$v(t) = At + C \qquad (3.61)$$

We can see that Eq. (3.61) is just as correct as Eq. (3.60) by differentiating both sides of Eq. (3.61) and Eq. (3.60); both equations then give back Eq. (3.55) stating that (dv/dt) equals A. It is common in physics to use the form Eq. (3.61), in which the constant of integration is on the side of the explicit integral, which, in Eq. (3.61), is At.

Eq. (3.61) gives us the result we have been seeking because it gives the velocity as a function $v(t)$ of the time. Eq. (3.61) says that the velocity equals the constant magnitude A of the acceleration times the time t, plus the constant of integration C. From what has been said so far, the value of C is undetermined; C can be any constant. If what has been given so far is all the information available, then Eq. (3.61) is

80 CALCULUS FOR PHYSICS

as complete a solution as possible of the problem as posed. We are unable to say anything more about the constant C.

However, in many physics problems, we are given additional information which allows us to determine the value of the constant of integration. For example, suppose we are considering the motion of the particle described above and that we are given the value of the particle's velocity at the instant of time $t = 0$. We will use the symbol $v(0)$ for the velocity of the particle at $t = 0$. This symbol is just what we obtain by putting $t = 0$ in the functional notation $v(t)$, so $v(0)$ means the value of $v(t)$ when $t = 0$. Let's consider Eq. (3.61) at the instant of time $t = 0$ by setting $t = 0$ in Eq. (3.61). The result is

$$v(0) = C \qquad (3.62)$$

Eq. (3.62) says that the constant of integration C is equal to $v(0)$, the value of the velocity of the particle when $t = 0$. Putting Eq. (3.62) into Eq. (3.61) gives

$$v(t) = v(0) + At \qquad (3.63)$$

Eq. (3.63) says that $v(t)$, the particle's velocity at time t, equals the quantity At plus $v(0)$, the particle's velocity at time $t = 0$. We see that the description in Eq. (3.63) of the velocity $v(t)$ as a function of time is more complete than the description in Eq. (3.61) in which the constant C was undetermined. Often in physics problems, some information is known which allows us to determine the value of the constant of integration involved. In the example just discussed, that information was the value of $v(0)$, the velocity at the instant $t = 0$. Since $t = 0$ is the instant at which the motion of the particle begins, knowledge of something (such as the velocity) at $t = 0$ is referred to as an *initial condition* for the problem. Thus a knowledge of the value of the initial velocity $v(0)$ is an initial condition for the problem of the moving particle.

Let's consider a numerical example for concreteness. Suppose a ball is thrown vertically downward with an initial velocity of 10 meters per second. We want to find the ball's velocity as a function of time. We will use the symbol $v_y(t)$ for the velocity of the ball in the vertical (y) direction. We saw in Chap. 2 that the acceleration of the ball (neglecting air resistance) is downward with the magnitude

$$a = 9.8 \text{ meters per second per second} \qquad (3.64)$$

and where we consider the downward vertical direction positive, so a is positive. From the definition of acceleration, we have

$$\frac{dv_y}{dt} = a = 9.8 \qquad (3.65)$$

where we omit explicit mention of the units in Eq. (3.65). Rewriting Eq. (3.65) in terms of differentials gives

$$dv_y = 9.8\, dt \qquad (3.66)$$

Integrating Eq. (3.66) with respect to time yields

$$v_y(t) = 9.8t + C \qquad (3.67)$$

Setting $t = 0$ in Eq. (3.67) gives us

$$v_y(0) = C \qquad (3.68)$$

Eq. (3.68) says that the constant of integration C is equal to $v_y(0)$, the value of the vertical velocity at $t = 0$. In other words, C is equal to the *initial* ($t = 0$) *velocity* of the ball. Since we are given that the initial velocity is 10 meters per second, Eq. (3.68) becomes

$$C = 10 \text{ meters per second} \qquad (3.69)$$

Note in Eq. (3.69) that the initial velocity of 10 meters per second downward has a positive sign because we are considering the downward vertical direction as positive. Substituting Eq. (3.69) into Eq. (3.67) gives

$$v_y(t) = 10 + 9.8t \qquad (3.70)$$

Eq. (3.70) gives the downward vertical velocity $v_y(t)$ as a function of time. We can calculate v_y at any instant of time by substituting that value of t into Eq. (3.70). For example, when $t = 2$ seconds, the velocity of the ball is given by

$$v_y(2) = 10 + 9.8(2) = 29.6 \text{ meters per second} \qquad (3.71)$$

We note also that Eq. (3.70) is, of course, of just the same form as the general result in Eq. (3.63). If we substitute $A = 9.8$ meters per second per second and $v(0) = v_y(0) = 10$ meters per second into the general result in Eq. (3.63), we obtain Eq. (3.70) describing our numerical example.

To recapitulate, we have seen that a knowledge of an initial condition enables us to determine the constant of integration in the kinematics problem we have been discussing. This is generally true in problems in which time is the independent variable, as it so frequently is in physics. One initial condition (like the value of the velocity) known at the initial instant $t = 0$ of the motion allows us to determine one constant of integration. Some problems involve two integrations and hence involve two constants of integration. In such a case, it is necessary to know two initial conditions in order to determine the two constants of integration.

It is useful at this point to make a graph of Eq. (3.63) giving the velocity $v(t)$ as a function of time t; this graph is shown in Fig. 3.1. If we examine Eq. (3.63), repeated below for convenience,

$$v(t) = v(0) + At \qquad (3.63)$$

we see that it is of the form

$$y = b + mx \qquad (1.39)$$

the equation of a straight line, seen earlier in Eq. (1.39), of slope m and intercept b. Comparing Eq. (1.39) and Eq. (3.63), we see that a graph of $v(t)$ as a function of time t is a straight line of slope A and of intercept $v(0)$ on the v axis. These features are shown in Fig. 3.1. Since the derivative gives the slope of the curve, we calculate

$$\frac{dv}{dt} = A \qquad (3.72)$$

from Eq. (3.63), showing that the straight line in Fig. 3.1 has a slope equal to A. Since we were given that A is a constant, the slope is

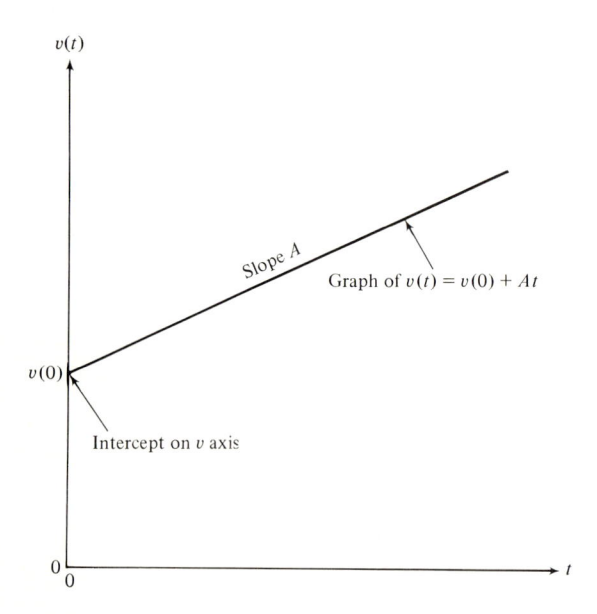

Figure 3.1 Graph of the straight line $v(t) = v(0) + At$, of slope A and intercept $v(0)$ on the v axis, plotted as a function of t.

SUMS AND INTEGRALS **83**

constant, as it should be for a straight line. The intercept on the vertical velocity axis is $v(0)$, the value of the velocity when the time $t = 0$. The intercept on the v axis in Fig. 3.1 is thus the initial velocity, that is, the velocity at $t = 0$.

In our discussion so far of constants of integration, we considered a problem in which the independent variable was the time. While this is a very important type of problem in physics, we will sometimes integrate over a variable other than the time. Consider the following example. Suppose we know that the derivative (dy/dx) of a function $y(x)$ is equal to $(x/2)$, so

$$\frac{dy}{dx} = \frac{x}{2} \tag{3.73}$$

and, in addition, we know that the function $y(x)$ has the value 1 when $x = 0$, so

$$y(0) = 1 \tag{3.74}$$

We wish to find the function $y(x)$. From Eq. (3.73), we have the differential dy as

$$dy = \tfrac{1}{2}x\, dx \tag{3.75}$$

Integrating Eq. (3.75) gives us

$$y = \int dy = \int \tfrac{1}{2}x\, dx = \tfrac{1}{4}x^2 \tag{3.76}$$

so, adding a constant of integration, we have

$$y(x) = \tfrac{1}{4}x^2 + C \tag{3.77}$$

We can use the information contained in the condition in Eq. (3.74) to determine the constant of integration C. To find $y(0)$, the value of y when $x = 0$, we substitute $x = 0$ into Eq. (3.77), obtaining

$$y(0) = C \tag{3.78}$$

Eqs. (3.78) and (3.74) together tell us that

$$C = 1 \tag{3.79}$$

so the condition that $y = 1$ when $x = 0$ determines the value of the constant C as equal to 1. Then, from Eq. (3.77),

$$y(x) = \tfrac{1}{4}x^2 + 1 \tag{3.80}$$

is the complete form of the function $y(x)$. This function is a parabola passing through the point $(0, 1)$ and is shown in Fig. 2.12 of Chap. 2.

84 CALCULUS FOR PHYSICS

In both of the examples in this section, we were given the derivative of a function and found the function by integration. In both cases, we were also given an additional condition or piece of information that enabled us to determine the value of the constant of integration in the problem. In the example in which time was the independent variable, we were told the value of the desired function (the velocity) at the initial instant ($t = 0$) of the problem; this is called an initial condition. In the second example, we were again given the value of the function $y(x)$ at some value of the independent variable x and this condition allowed us to determine the constant of integration.

Exercises

3.6 A particle moves with constant velocity in a straight line in one direction. The value of its constant velocity is V meters per second and the distance s it has moved is 100 meters at the initial instant of time $t = 0$. Find the equation giving s as a function of time.

3.7 The derivative of a certain function $y(x)$ is given by

$$\frac{dy}{dx} = 6 - 2x$$

and it is known that $y = 9$ when $x = 3$. Find the function $y(x)$.

3.8 A certain particle is moving with a constant acceleration equal to zero, and its initial velocity at $t = 0$ has the value 100 meters per second. Find the equation for the particle's velocity as a function of time.

SUMMATION NOTATION

We digress briefly at this point to introduce a useful notation for writing sums. Suppose we have a sum of terms, such as

$$a_1 + a_2 + a_3 + a_4 \tag{3.81}$$

where the a's can be anything—numbers, functions, etc. (The terms in Eq. (3.81) are read a sub-one, a sub-two, etc.). The sum of terms in Eq. (3.81) can be written as

$$\sum_{i=1}^{4} a_i \tag{3.82}$$

where the Σ (the Greek letter capital sigma) is called a summation symbol. In the expression (3.82), the letter "i" is called the index and, by definition, it takes on all of the integral values from the value written under the Σ (in this case, 1) to the value written above the Σ

(in this case, 4). Thus, the index i has the values 1, 2, 3, 4, so the expression (3.82) is

$$\sum_{i=1}^{4} a_i = a_1 + a_2 + a_3 + a_4 \qquad (3.83)$$

You will frequently see a sum of terms written as

$$\sum_{i=1}^{n} b_i \qquad (3.84)$$

The "n" above the Σ means that the index i takes on integral values $1, 2, \ldots$ up to some value n. The sum in Eq. (3.84) would thus be

$$b_1 + b_2 + \cdots + b_n \qquad (3.85)$$

indicating that the last term in the sum is the one for which the index i is equal to n.

Note that the index i is called a *dummy* index because it doesn't matter what symbol is used for the index since

$$\sum_{i=1}^{4} a_i = \sum_{k=1}^{4} a_k = a_1 + a_2 + a_3 + a_4 \qquad (3.86)$$

The symbol used for the index in the sum in Eq. (3.86) is immaterial.

A sum which will be useful to us later is

$$\sum_{i=1}^{n} f(x_i) = f(x_1) + f(x_2) + \cdots + f(x_n) \qquad (3.87)$$

where $f(x)$ is some function of the variable x. In Eq. (3.87), $f(x_1)$ is the value of the function $f(x)$ at the point $x = x_1$, and so on. The sum Eq. (3.87) is thus a sum of the values of the function $f(x)$ at the points $x = x_1$, $x = x_2$, and so on up to $x = x_n$.

Exercises

3.9 Write the following sums using the summation symbol:

(a) $x_1^2 + x_2^2 + x_3^2 + x_4^2$; (b) $1 + y + y^2 + y^3 + y^4 + y^5$; (c) $1^2 + 2^2 + 3^2$.

REVIEW OF THE DEFINITION OF THE DEFINITE INTEGRAL

We now *review* the definition of the definite integral on the assumption that you will refresh your memory, on any points about which you may be rusty, by using your calculus book. The definite integral is

86 CALCULUS FOR PHYSICS

extremely important in physics and is the second major concern (with the derivative) of this book. The definition will aim to be simple rather than the most general and rigorous possible.

Consider a function $f(x)$ in the interval $a \leq x \leq b$ shown in Fig. 3.2. Suppose we subdivide the interval between $x = a$ and $x = b$ into n subintervals of equal length. (It is convenient, but not necessary, that the subintervals be of equal length.) The subdivision is accomplished by inserting the $(n - 1)$ intermediate points $x_1, x_2, \ldots, x_{n-1}$ shown in Fig. 3.2. We will give the point $x = a$ the label x_0 and give the point $x = b$ the label x_n. Thus there are $(n + 1)$ points x_k indicated, where $k = 0, 1, 2, \ldots, n$.

Next, we choose a point in each subinterval. While this point may be chosen in any way we like, in the interests of simplicity of visualization, we choose this point to be in the center of each subinterval. We give the chosen point in the subinterval between x_0 and x_1 the label c_1; we give the chosen point in the subinterval between x_1 and x_2 the label c_2, and so on. Thus c_k is the chosen point in the center of the subinterval between x_{k-1} and x_k. The length of the subinterval between x_{k-1} and x_k will be denoted by Δx_k, where

$$\Delta x_k = x_k - x_{k-1} \qquad (3.88)$$

Next, we find the value of the function $f(x)$ at each of the n chosen points within the n subintervals: $f(c_1)$ is the value of the function f at the point $x = c_1$, $f(c_2)$ is the value of f at the point $x = c_2$, and so on through $f(c_n)$, the value of f at the point $x = c_n$. Then we construct the *sum*

$$f(c_1)\Delta x_1 + f(c_2)\Delta x_2 + \cdots + f(c_{n-1})\Delta x_{n-1} + f(c_n)\Delta x_n$$
$$(3.89)$$

which may be written using the summation notation as

$$\sum_{k=1}^{n} f(c_k)\Delta x_k \qquad (3.90)$$

The sum in Eq. (3.90) thus has n terms, one for each of the n subintervals between $x = a$ and $x = b$.

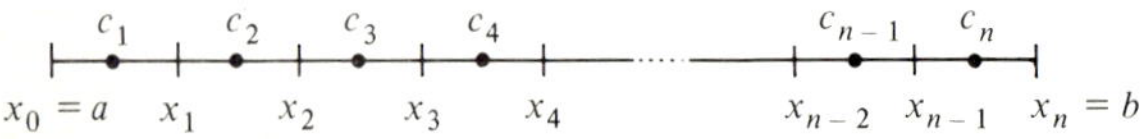

Figure 3.2 Subdivision of the interval $a \leq x \leq b$ into n subintervals by the $(n - 1)$ points $x_1, x_2, \ldots, x_{n-1}$. In each subinterval, of length $\Delta x_k = x_k - x_{k-1}$, a point c_k is chosen as shown. For example, in the second subinterval, between x_2 and x_1, the point chosen is $x = c_2$.

Consider a sequence of sums of the form in Eq. (3.90). These sums are constructed by dividing the interval $a \leq x \leq b$ into a larger and larger number of subintervals of decreasing length. Thus, we are considering a sequence of sums like those in Eq. (3.90) as the number n of subintervals gets very large and the length Δx_k of each subinterval gets very small. We are therefore taking the *limit* of the sum in Eq. (3.90) as the length Δx_k of the subintervals gets very small, a process we indicate by writing $\Delta x_k \to 0$. (In this book we assume that this limit will always exist in the cases in which we are interested.) The limit approached by the sum in Eq. (3.90) is a *number* which we denote by A, so we have

$$\lim_{\Delta x_k \to 0} \sum_{k=1}^{n} f(c_k) \Delta x_k = A \tag{3.91}$$

By definition, the number A is called the *definite integral* of the function $f(x)$ from $x = a$ to $x = b$. The definite integral A is denoted by

$$A \equiv \int_a^b f(x)\, dx \tag{3.92}$$

In expression (3.92), the number a is the *lower limit* of integration, the number b is the *upper limit* of integration, and the symbol x is called the *variable* of integration.

The preceding is the formal definition of the definite integral as the limit of a sum. The definition will become clearer and more readily visualized when we discuss the geometric interpretation and applications of the definite integral. First, however, we must discuss the evaluation of definite integrals.

EVALUATION OF DEFINITE INTEGRALS

Given the definition (3.91) of the definite integral of the function $f(x)$ from a to b, how do we evaluate it? The answer is supplied by the fundamental theorem of integral calculus, which, in simplified form, is as follows. Suppose $f(x)$ is a continuous function in the interval $a \leq x \leq b$, and is the derivative of another function $F(x)$, so

$$\frac{dF(x)}{dx} = f(x) \tag{3.93}$$

Then it follows that

$$dF(x) = f(x)\, dx \tag{3.94}$$

88 CALCULUS FOR PHYSICS

and

$$F(x) = \int f(x)\, dx \qquad (3.95)$$

meaning that $F(x)$ is an indefinite integral of $f(x)$. The fundamental theorem then asserts that the definite integral of $f(x)$ from $x = a$ to $x = b$ is given by

$$\int_a^b f(x)\, dx = F(b) - F(a) \qquad (3.96)$$

Eq. (3.96) says that, to obtain the definite integral of $f(x)$, we find the indefinite integral $F(x)$ from Eq. (3.95) and then evaluate $F(x)$ at $x = b$ and at $x = a$.

Consider an example; let's calculate

$$\int_1^2 x\, dx \qquad (3.97)$$

so the function $f(x) = x$, $b = 2$, and $a = 1$. We find $F(x)$ as the indefinite integral

$$F(x) = \int x\, dx = \frac{x^2}{2} \qquad (3.98)$$

so

$$F(2) = \frac{2^2}{2} = 2;\ F(1) = \frac{1^2}{2} = \frac{1}{2} \qquad (3.99)$$

and the desired definite integral is

$$\int_1^2 x\, dx = F(2) - F(1) = 2 - \frac{1}{2} = \frac{3}{2} \qquad (3.100)$$

Note that it is not necessary to consider a constant of integration in the indefinite integral in Eq. (3.98)

A common notation for the quantity $F(b) - F(a)$ is the following:

$$[F(x)]_a^b \equiv F(b) - F(a) \qquad (3.101)$$

so Eq. (3.96) can also be written as

$$\int_a^b f(x)\, dx = [F(x)]_a^b \qquad (3.102)$$

where, again, the relation between $F(x)$ and $f(x)$ is given by Eq. (3.93), that is, $f(x) = dF(x)/dx$.

Consider another example. We will evaluate

$$\int_0^{\pi/2} \cos x\, dx \qquad (3.103)$$

From our results above,

$$\int_0^{\pi/2} \cos x \, dx = [\sin x]_0^{\pi/2} = \sin \frac{\pi}{2} - \sin 0 = 1 \quad (3.104)$$

Note that the variable of integration in a definite integral is a *dummy* variable in the mathematical sense. This means that the *value* of the definite integral (which is just a number) does not depend on the variable of integration. For example,

$$\int_0^{\pi/2} \cos x \, dx = 1; \quad \int_0^{\pi/2} \cos \theta \, d\theta = 1; \quad \int_0^{\pi/2} \cos z \, dz = 1 \quad (3.105)$$

All three definite integrals in Eq. (3.105) have the same value, namely unity.

We close this section with two important and useful properties of definite integrals. First, it is true that

$$\int_b^a f(x) \, dx = -\int_a^b f(x) \, dx \quad (3.106)$$

Eq. (3.106) tells us that interchanging the limits of integration in a definite integral multiplies the integral by (-1). Second,

$$\int_a^b f(x) \, dx = \int_a^c f(x) \, dx + \int_c^b f(x) \, dx \quad (3.107)$$

In Eq. (3.107), it is not necessary that the point c be between the points a and b.

Exercises

3.10 Evaluate $\int_0^\pi \sin x \, dx$.

3.11 Evaluate $\int_0^2 x^2 \, dx$.

3.12 Evaluate $\int_0^\infty e^{-x} \, dx$.

3.13 Evaluate $\int_0^a (x - a)^2 \, dx$, where a is a constant.

3.14 Evaluate $\int_\infty^b x^{-2} \, dx$, where b is a constant.

3.15 Evaluate $\int_0^a \dfrac{x \, dx}{(d^2 + x^2)^{1/2}}$ where d and a are constants.

GEOMETRIC INTERPRETATION OF THE DEFINITE INTEGRAL

We now consider the *geometric* meaning of the definite integral. This interpretation will provide a concrete and visual meaning for the integral which will pave the way for the physical applications in which we are primarily interested.

90 CALCULUS FOR PHYSICS

We return to the sum in Eq. (3.90)

$$\sum_{k=1}^{n} f(c_k)\,\Delta x_k \qquad (3.90)$$

on which the definition (3.91) of the definite integral is based, and look into its geometric interpretation in a specific case. Consider the graph of the function $f(x)$, as a function of x, shown in Fig. 3.3, between $x = a$ and $x = b$. We divide the interval $a \leq x \leq b$ on the x axis into four subintervals of equal length by inserting three points x_1, x_2, x_3 between the points $x_0 = a$ and $x_4 = b$. The lengths of the four subintervals are equal, so

$$\Delta x_1 = (x_1 - x_0) = \Delta x_2 = (x_2 - x_1) = \cdots = \Delta x_4 = (x_4 - x_3)$$
$$(3.108)$$

We will denote the length of each subinterval by Δx, so

$$\Delta x \equiv \Delta x_1 = \Delta x_2 = \Delta x_3 = \Delta x_4 \qquad (3.109)$$

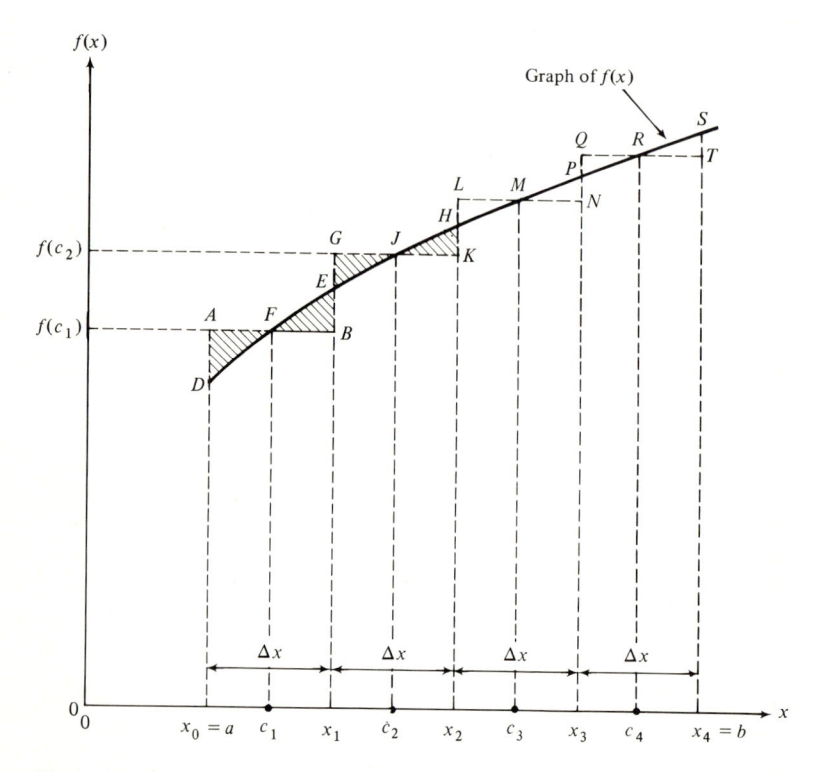

Figure 3.3 The area between the graph of the function $f(x)$ and the x axis, between $x = a$ and $x = b$, divided into four rectangles, each of width Δx.

SUMS AND INTEGRALS 91

We choose a point in the center of each subinterval: these are the points $x = c_1$; $x = c_2$; $x = c_3$; $x = c_4$ shown in Fig. 3.3.
Next, we construct the sum

$$\sum_{k=1}^{4} f(c_k) \Delta x_k = f(c_1) \Delta x_1 + f(c_2) \Delta x_2 + f(c_3) \Delta x_3 + f(c_4) \Delta x_4$$

(3.110)

Since all of the Δx_k's are, from Eq. (3.109), equal to Δx, the sum in Eq. (3.110) becomes

$$\sum_{k=1}^{4} f(c_k) \Delta x = f(c_1) \Delta x + f(c_2) \Delta x + f(c_3) \Delta x + f(c_4) \Delta x$$

(3.111)

We now want to give a geometric interpretation to each of the four terms of the form $[f(c_k) \Delta x]$ in the sum in Eq. (3.111).

As seen in Fig. 3.3, the quantity $[f(c_1) \Delta x]$ is the area of the rectangle $(aABx_1)$. The quantity $[f(c_2) \Delta x]$ is the area of the rectangle $(x_1 GKx_2)$, and so on for the other two rectangles $(x_2 LNx_3)$ and $(x_3 QTx_4)$ in the figure. The sum in Eq. (3.111) thus is the sum of the areas of the four vertical rectangles, centered at c_1, c_2, c_3, c_4, in Fig. 3.3. Consider the rectangle $(aABx_1)$ centered at $x = c_1$. We assert that the area $(aABx_1)$ is approximately equal to the irregularly shaped area $(aDFEx_1)$. In other words, we say

Area of $(aABx_1) \cong$ area of $(aDFEx_1)$ (3.112)

by assuming that the shaded area DAF is approximately equal to the shaded area FEB and that these two shaded areas "cancel each other out," thereby making the statement in Eq. (3.112) correct. The rectangle $(aABx_1)$ has an area $[f(c_1) \Delta x]$ where $f(c_1)$ is the height of the rectangle and Δx is its width. From Eq. (3.112), we conclude

$$f(c_1) \Delta x \cong \text{area of } (aDFEx_1)$$ (3.113)

meaning that the irregular area $(aDFEx_1)$ is approximately equal to the area $f(c_1) \Delta x$ of the rectangle of $aABx_1$. For convenience of notation, we denote the area of $(aDFEx_1)$ by A_1, so we have, from Eq. (3.113),

$$A_1 \cong f(c_1) \Delta x$$ (3.114)

for the area A_1 of the irregular shape $(aDFEx_1)$. Similarly, the area A_2 of the irregular shape $(x_1 EJHx_2)$ is approximately equal to the area $[f(c_2) \Delta x]$ of the rectangle $(x_1 GKx_2)$, so we have

$$A_2 \cong f(c_2) \Delta x$$ (3.115)

92 CALCULUS FOR PHYSICS

In the same way we have, for the areas A_3 and A_4 of the shapes (x_2HMPx_3) and (x_3PRSb), that

$$A_3 \cong f(c_3)\Delta x \tag{3.116}$$

$$A_4 \cong f(c_4)\Delta x \tag{3.117}$$

The sum of A_1 to A_4 is the area $(aDSb)$ contained between the curve of $f(x)$ and the x axis from $x = a$ to $x = b$. Denoting this area $(aDSb)$ by A, we have

$$A = A_1 + A_2 + A_3 + A_4 \tag{3.118}$$

or

$$A \cong f(c_1)\Delta x + f(c_2)\Delta x + f(c_3)\Delta x + f(c_4)\Delta x \tag{3.119}$$

which is just the sum in Eq. (3.111). We conclude that the area A contained between the curve $f(x)$ and the x axis between $x = a$ and $x = b$ is given approximately by the sum in Eq. (3.111), so

$$A \cong \sum_{k=1}^{4} f(c_k)\Delta x \tag{3.120}$$

The content of Eq. (3.120), relating the area A between the curve $f(x)$ and the x axis to the sum in Eq. (3.111), is the basis for the geometric interpretation of the definite integral. This area is often referred to as the "area under the curve of the function $f(x)$."

It is intuitively clear from Fig. 3.3 that the approximation expressed by Eq. (3.120) becomes better as the number of rectangles is increased. In other words, a better approximation to the area under the curve in Fig. 3.3 is obtained by using a larger number of narrower rectangles. Using narrower rectangles is achieved by letting the width Δx of each rectangle become smaller. In the limit as Δx becomes very small, the number n of terms of the form $f(c_k)\Delta x$ in the sum in Eq. (3.120) increases, so we are taking the *limit* of the sum in Eq. (3.90),

$$A = \lim_{\Delta x \to 0} \sum_{k=1}^{n} f(c_k)\Delta x \tag{3.121}$$

as $\Delta x \to 0$ and as $n \to \infty$. In the limit as $\Delta x \to 0$ in Eq. (3.121), the area A becomes *exactly* the area under the curve. Thus the limit of the sum in Eq. (3.121) is exactly the area between the curve of $f(x)$ and the x axis between $x = a$ and $x = b$. But from Eqs. (3.91) and (3.92), the limit of the sum in Eq. (3.121) is just the definite integral of $f(x)$ from $x = a$ to $x = b$. We therefore conclude that the definite integral

$$\int_a^b f(x)\,dx \tag{3.122}$$

is exactly equal to the area A between the graph of the function $f(x)$ and the x axis between $x = a$ and $x = b$.

Let's illustrate this result with the concrete example in Fig. 3.4, which shows the graph of the function

$$f(x) = x^2 + 1 \qquad (3.123)$$

in the interval $0 \leq x \leq 4$. We will calculate the area A, shown shaded in the figure, between the curve of $f(x)$ and the x axis from $x = 1$ to $x = 3$. From the discussion above, the area A is

$$A = \int_1^3 f(x)\, dx = \int_1^3 (x^2 + 1)\, dx \qquad (3.124)$$

We evaluate the definite integral in Eq. (3.124) as

$$\int_1^3 (x^2 + 1)\, dx = \left[\frac{x^3}{3} + x\right]_1^3 = \left[\frac{3^3}{3} + 3 - \frac{1^3}{3} - 1\right] = 10\frac{2}{3} \qquad (3.125)$$

The shaded area is thus $10(2/3)$ units of area. (If length on the graph in Fig. 3.4 is in meters, the area will be in square meters, etc. Since usually no unit of length is specified in drawings like Fig. 3.4, we just say the area is so many units of area.)

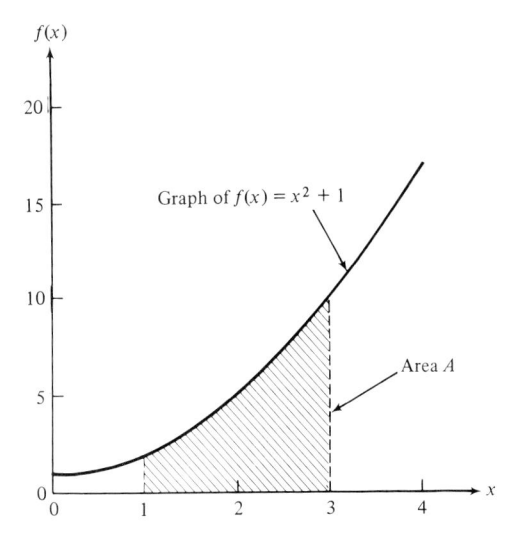

Figure 3.4 Area A between the graph of the function $f(x) = x^2 + 1$ and the x axis between $x = 1$ and $x = 3$. The area A is shaded.

Exercises

3.16 Calculate the area between the graph of $y = f(x) = 2x + 1$ and the x axis between $x = 1$ and $x = 2$.

3.17 Express in your own words the interpretation of Eq. (3.107) in terms of areas for the case in which $a < c < b$.

3.18 Consider a function $p(V)$ of an independent variable V, where

$$p(V) = \frac{C}{V}$$

and C is a positive constant. Calculate the area under the curve of $p(V)$ between the point $V = V_1$ and $V = V_2$, where $V_2 > V_1$.

INTERPRETATION OF THE DEFINITE INTEGRAL AS A "SUM OF INFINITESIMAL ELEMENTS"

We now reconsider the definite integral as the area A under a curve in a somewhat different way. We have just seen that the area A is the limit of the sum in Eq. (3.91) as $\Delta x_k \to 0$ and this limit is defined as the definite integral in Eq. (3.92). Thus we have

$$A = \lim_{\Delta x_k \to 0} \sum_{k=1}^{n} f(c_k) \Delta x_k = \int_a^b f(x)\, dx \qquad (3.126)$$

where $a \leq x \leq b$. We will now construct the definite integral giving the area A under the curve $f(x)$ in a different manner. This approach omits the sum and limit in Eq. (3.126) and constructs the integral for the area directly. While this approach is mathematically rather casual, it is very useful and is used constantly in physics.

Consider the graph of the function $f(x)$ for $a \leq x \leq b$ shown in Fig. 3.5, and consider the shaded area in the figure. This shaded area is a vertical strip of width dx, where dx is the differential of x, the independent variable. The geometric interpretation of dx in Fig. 3.5 is that dx is a very small ("infinitesimal") length along the x axis. The shaded strip is located at some point $x = x'$ on the x axis, and we denote the area of the strip by dA. The geometric interpretation of the differential dA is that dA is the very small ("infinitesimal") area of the shaded strip. We will call dA an *infinitesimal element of area* under the curve of $f(x)$. Similarly, we call dx an *infinitesimal element of length* along the x axis.

The area of the element is dA. The area dA is equal to the area of a rectangle of width dx and height $f(x')$, where $f(x')$ is the value of the function $f(x)$ at the point $x = x'$ at which the element is located. We have

$$dA = f(x')\,dx \qquad (3.127)$$

Since x' can be *any* point x between $x = a$ and $x = b$, we can drop the prime on x', and write Eq. (3.127) as

$$dA = f(x)\,dx \qquad (3.128)$$

where dA is the area of the infinitesimal element of area located at the point x. We note from Eq. (3.128) that the area dA of the element *depends on* x. To emphasize that fact, we write Eq. (3.128) as

$$dA(x) = f(x)\,dx \qquad (3.129)$$

an equation that says that the area $dA(x)$ of an element of area depends on the point x at which it is located. This is seen in Fig. 3.6, which shows two elements, both of the same width dx, but with different areas, located at two different points on the x axis. The reason that the area of the element of area $dA(x)$ depends on x is because the function $f(x)$ in Eq. (3.129) has different values at different points x on the x axis.

Now that we have the element of area $dA(x)$ we may calculate the *total* area A under the curve by *adding up* the areas of all of the elements between $x = a$ and $x = b$ in Fig. 3.6. We "add up" the areas of all the elements by *integrating* $dA(x)$, which depends on x, between $x = a$ and $x = b$. Thus we have

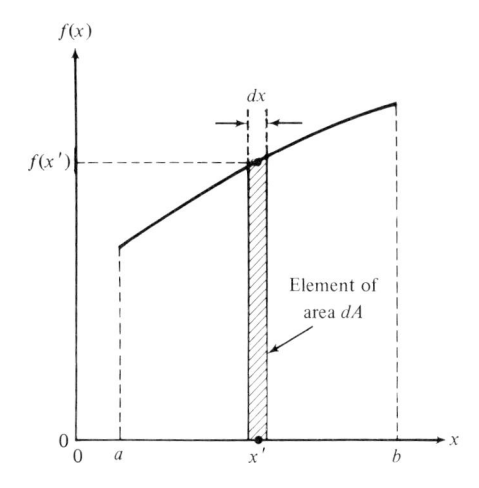

$$A = \int_a^b dA(x) \qquad (3.130)$$

Figure 3.5 Graph of the function $f(x)$ for $a \leq x \leq b$, showing the infinitesimal element of area dA as the shaded strip. The element of area is located at the point $x = x'$.

96 CALCULUS FOR PHYSICS

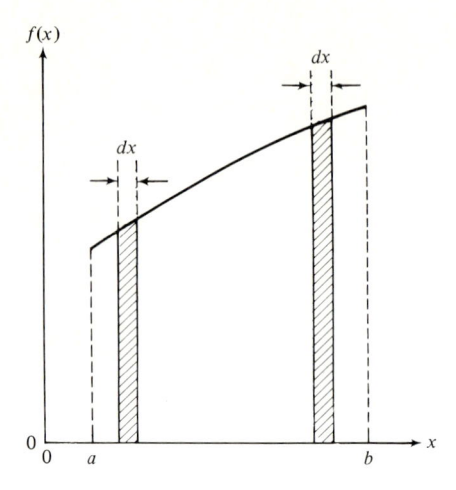

Figure 3.6 Graph of the function $f(x)$ showing elements of area $dA(x) = f(x)\,dx$ at two different points on the x axis.

where in Eq. (3.130), the variable of integration is x because the area $dA(x)$ of each element is a function of x.

Keep in mind that, in our calculation of the area A under the curve in the preceding section, we took the limit of the sum in Eq. (3.91) as $\Delta x \to 0$ and arrived at the definite integral (3.92). Here we have "replaced the sum by an integral," as in Eq. (3.130). You will see that phrase often in physics. We now substitute Eq. (3.129) for $dA(x)$ into Eq. (3.130), obtaining

$$A = \int_a^b f(x)\,dx \qquad (3.131)$$

for the area A under the curve of $f(x)$ for $a \leq x \leq b$. Eq. (3.131) for the area A as the definite integral is just the result we obtained by the more precise process of taking the limit of the sum.

The procedure, described above, of adding up infinitesimal elements of some quantity by integrating, is much used in physics. In the discussion above, we added up elements of area to get the total area under a curve, but the infinitesimal elements can be elements of many quantities of physical interest. The next section of this chapter will describe several examples of this procedure.

Let's re-do the example in the preceding section by the procedure of adding up or integrating elements of area. We found earlier the area between the graph of

$$f(x) = x^2 + 1 \qquad (3.132)$$

and the x axis between $x = 1$ and $x = 3$. The curve in Fig. 3.7 shows

SUMS AND INTEGRALS 97

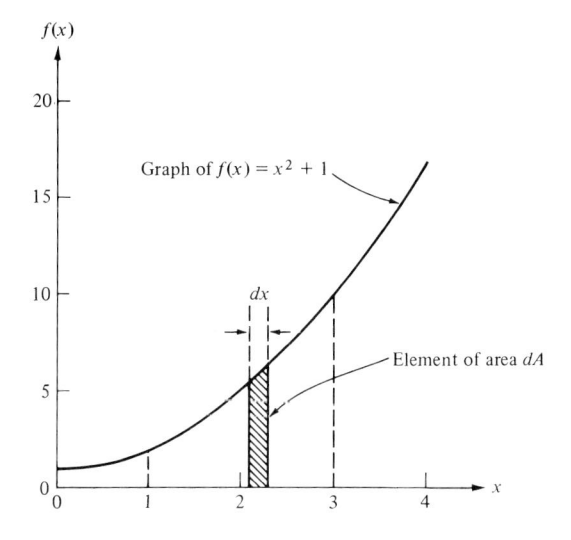

Figure 3.7 Graph of the function $f(x) = x^2 + 1$ showing an element of area dA.

the graph of the function and an element of area dA, where

$$dA(x) = f(x)\, dx = (x^2 + 1)\, dx \qquad (3.133)$$

so the element of area $dA(x)$ depends on x. We find the total area A by integrating $dA(x)$, so

$$A = \int dA(x) = \int_1^3 (x^2 + 1)\, dx \qquad (3.134)$$

In Eq. (3.134), the variable of integration is x, and we want the area between $x = 1$ and $x = 3$, so those are the limits of integration. In this way, by adding up elements of area, we arrive at the same definite integral for the area under the curve that we found earlier in Eq. (3.124).

Let's conclude this section with another geometric example of a calculation in which we add up infinitesimal elements by integrating. We will calculate the circumference C of a circle of radius r. We recall from Chap. 1 that the arc length s, subtending an angle θ (in radians) in a circle of radius r, is, from Eq. (1.47), given by

$$s = r\theta \qquad (3.135)$$

We take differentials of both sides of (3.135), obtaining

$$ds = r\,d\theta \qquad (3.136)$$

because the radius r of a circle is a constant. The geometric significance of ds in Eq. (3.136) is that ds is a small length of arc along the circumference, as shown in Fig. 3.8. We call ds an infinitesimal element of arc length along the circumference. The element of arc length ds subtends an infinitesimal angle $d\theta$, also shown in Fig. 3.8. Note that the infinitesimal element ds is located at some value of the angle θ, which is measured so that $\theta = 0$ at the horizontal axis. (This is exactly analogous to the element of area dA being located at some point on the x axis in Fig. 3.5.) Note that, in Eq. (3.136), the element ds does *not* depend on θ because r is a constant and not a function of θ. Hence the element ds in this example is constant in magnitude (unlike the element of area $dA(x) = f(x)\,dx$ we discussed previously).

The value of the circumference C is the total arc length, all around the circumference of the circle, so we add up all the elements of arc length ds by integrating. We get

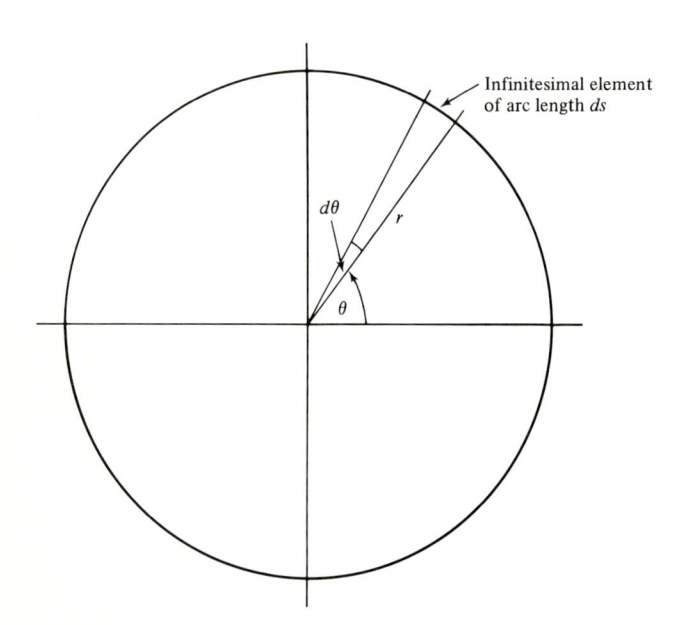

$$C = \int ds \qquad (3.137)$$

Figure 3.8 An element of arc length ds subtending an infinitesimal angle $d\theta$ in a circle of radius r. The angle θ, measured from the horizontal, locates the position of $d\theta$, and, hence, of ds.

Using Eq. (3.136), thus becomes

$$C = \int r\, d\theta = r \int d\theta \qquad (3.138)$$

an integral in which the variable of integration is the angle θ shown in Fig. 3.8. To evaluate the integral in Eq. (3.138), we need to know the limits of the definite integral, that is, the range of values over which the variable of integration θ varies in the problem. We can see from Fig. 3.8 that, in order to trace out the entire circumference of the circle, θ must vary from 0 radians to 2π radians, so

$$0 \le \theta \le 2\pi \qquad (3.139)$$

is the range of values of θ. The lower limit of the integral is 0 and the upper limit is 2π. The complete integral for the circumference C is thus

$$C = r \int_0^{2\pi} d\theta \qquad (3.140)$$

Evaluating the integral in Eq. (3.140) gives

$$\int_0^{2\pi} d\theta = [\theta]_0^{2\pi} = [2\pi - 0] = 2\pi \qquad (3.141)$$

so we obtain

$$C = 2\pi r \qquad (3.142)$$

the familiar relation between the circumference C and the radius r of a circle.

The important point of this calculation of the circumference of a circle is the procedure by which it was done. In Eq. (3.137), we said that the length C of the circumference is obtained by integrating ("adding up") all of the infinitesimal elements of arc length ds. Once we had Eq. (3.137), we expressed the element of arc length ds as $r\,d\theta$ by using Eq. (3.135). This expressed ds in terms of the variable θ whose range of values we found in Eq. (3.139). Again, the essential thing we did was to "add up" or integrate the infinitesimal elements in the problem. This procedure is widely used in physics and is the subject of the next section of this chapter.

It is worth pointing out the mathematical similarity between the calculation of the area under the curve of $f(x) = x^2 + 1$ and the calculation of the circumference of the circle. In the former, when we said that the area A was the sum (integral) of the elements of area $dA(x)$, we wrote

$$A = \int dA(x) \qquad (3.143)$$

Then our next step was finding the element of area $dA(x)$ in terms of a variable of integration, which in that case was x, the distance along the x axis. This we did by calculating

$$dA(x) = f(x)\,dx = (x^2 + 1)\,dx \qquad (3.133)$$

in Eq. (3.133). The combination of Eqs. (3.143) and (3.133) allowed us to calculate A, the area we sought. In the calculation of the circumference C, we said C was the sum (integral) of the elements of arc length ds and wrote

$$C = \int ds \qquad (3.137)$$

Again, our next step was finding the element of arc length ds in terms of a variable of integration, which in this case was the angle θ in Fig. 3.8. This we did by calculating

$$ds = r\,d\theta \qquad (3.136)$$

Combining Eqs. (3.136) and (3.137) allowed us to calculate C in Eq. (3.140). Note that, in both cases, once we had set up the integral of the elements of the quantity of interest (area or arc length), the next step was to express that element in terms of a variable of integration. Sometimes that step is very simple (as in the case of calculating the area) or is more complicated (as in the case of the arc length). We will see a number of examples of varying degrees of complexity in the next section on physical applications of integration.

Exercises

3.19 Use the procedure of adding up infinitesimal elements of length by integration to calculate the length (distance) along the x axis from $x = a$ to $x = b$, where $b > a$.

3.20 Consider the straight line $f(x) = x$. Calculate, by integrating elements of area, the total area A between the graph of $f(x) = x$ and the x axis from $x = 0$ to $x = a$, where a is a constant.

PHYSICAL APPLICATIONS OF THE DEFINITE INTEGRAL

In this section, we will discuss a number of examples of the application of the definite integral to physics. The approach will be the same in each case—the addition of infinitesimal elements of some quantity by integration. The physics will be kept as simple as possible in order to emphasize the mathematical techniques, which, in this book, are the primary interest.

As our first example, we will discuss the work done by a force. We recall that, if a constant force F acts on a body and moves it a distance d, where the directions of the force and the distance are the same, then the work W done by the force is

$$W = Fd \qquad (3.144)$$

Eq. (3.144) assumes that the magnitude of the force F is constant. We now want to calculate the work done by a force whose magnitude is *variable* but whose direction is constant.

Consider, as shown in Fig. 3.9, a body being pulled along the x axis by a force F, were the directions of F and of the motion of the body are both along the x axis. Suppose, however, that the magnitude of F varies with position on the x axis, so the magnitude F of the force depends on the x coordinate of the body on which the force is exerted. We write this fact as

$$F = F(x) \qquad (3.145)$$

an equation which says that the magnitude F of the force is a function $F(x)$ of the x coordinate of the body. For example, when the body is at the point $x = x'$, then the magnitude of the force at that point is $F(x')$, and so on. Suppose the body is pulled along the x axis, starting at the point $x = x_s$ and finishing at the point $x = x_f$. How can we calculate the *total* amount of work W done by the force in moving the body from $x = x_s$ to $x = x_f$?

Since the magnitude of the force is *not* constant, we cannot just multiply force times the total distance moved as was done in Eq. (3.144). What we do to handle this situation of a variable force is the following. Consider Fig. 3.10, showing the x axis in the problem, and consider an infinitesimal element of length dx located at some point x on the x axis between x_s and x_f. Let us calculate the work done by the force in moving the body the infinitesimal distance dx located at point x. We denote this infinitesimal amount by work by dW. We next make the reasonable assumption that the magnitude of the force F is essentially constant over the very small distance dx, even though, strictly speaking, F varies with position on the x axis. At the point x

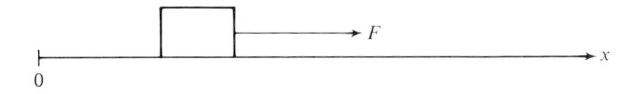

Figure 3.9 A force of magnitude F, in a direction parallel to the x axis, moving a body along the x axis.

where dx is located, the force F has the magnitude

$$F = F(x) \tag{3.146}$$

Since we're assuming that the magnitude of the force has the essentially constant value $F(x)$ over the infinitesimal length dx we're considering, we can calculate the infinitesimal amount of work dW by multiplying the magnitude of the force and the distance moved. The result is

$$dW = F(x)\,dx \tag{3.147}$$

where, to repeat, dW is the amount of work done by the force in moving the body the distance dx located at the point x. Note that, because $F(x)$ depends on x, dW depends on x. To emphasize that fact we rewrite Eq. (3.147) as

$$dW(x) = F(x)\,dx \tag{3.148}$$

To find the *total* work W done by the force in moving the body from x_s to x_f, we *add up* all of the infinitesimal elements (amounts) of work $dW(x)$, so we have

$$W = \int dW(x) \tag{3.149}$$

where, in Eq. (3.149), the variable of integration is x because $dW(x)$ depends on x. Eq. (3.149) says that the total work W is the sum of all of the infinitesimal amounts of work $dW(x)$ done by the force in moving the body the infinitesimal distances dx located at different points x on the x axis.

Then, from Eq. (3.148), we have the expression for $dW(x)$ in terms of $F(x)$ and dx, so Eq. (3.149) becomes

$$W = \int F(x)\,dx \tag{3.150}$$

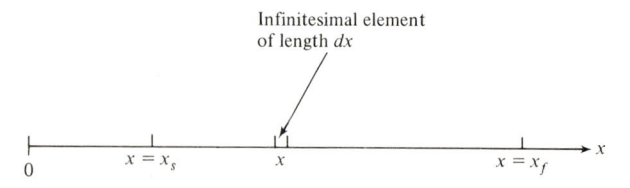

Figure 3.10 The x axis, showing an infinitesimal element of length dx located at the point x. The points $x = x_s$ and $x = x_f$ are, respectively, the starting and finishing points of the motion of the body.

where the variable of integration remains distance x because the integrand $F(x)$ depends on x. To find the limits of integration in Eq. (3.150), we know the body moves from its starting point $x = x_s$ to its final point $x = x_f$, so these values are the endpoints of the range of the variable of integration x. The value x_s is the lower limit and x_f is the upper limit in Eq. (3.150), which becomes

$$W = \int_{x_s}^{x_f} F(x)\, dx \qquad (3.151)$$

Eq. (3.151) gives the total work W done by the force $F(x)$, of variable magnitude, in moving the body from $x = x_s$ to $x = x_f$, assuming the directions of the force and the motion of the body are the same.

Eq. (3.151) is a general expression for any functional form $F(x)$ of the dependence of the force F on position x. In order to calculate the total work W using Eq. (3.151), one must know the particular function $F(x)$. As a specific example, let's consider that the force applied to the body is given by

$$F = F(x) = kx \qquad (3.152)$$

where k is a constant of proportionality. Eq. (3.152) says that the magnitude of the force F is proportional to the first power of the position coordinate x, so F varies linearly with x. Let's calculate the work W done by the force F given by Eq. (3.152) in moving the body from the point $x = 1$ to $x = 2$. Using Eq. (3.151), the starting point is $x = 1$ and the finishing point is $x = 2$, so W is given by

$$W = \int_1^2 kx\, dx \qquad (3.153)$$

We can evaluate the integral in Eq. (3.153). Our answer will be expressed in terms of the constant k, and Eq. (3.153) becomes

$$W = k\int_1^2 x\, dx = k\left[\frac{x^2}{2}\right]_1^2 = k\left[2 - \frac{1}{2}\right] = \frac{3k}{2} \qquad (3.154)$$

so the total work $W = (3k/2)$ units of work. (One would need to know the numerical value of k to obtain a numerical value of W.)

As a last point about this example, note that, in dealing with a physical problem, we assigned a physical interpretation (distance) to the mathematical variable of integration x in the problem. It is always useful to keep in mind the physical meaning of the mathematical symbols being used. Thus, in this example, when we integrate over the variable x, we would say we were "integrating over distance" because distance is the physical meaning of the variable x.

104 CALCULUS FOR PHYSICS

Our second example of the application of the definite integral comes from the field of heat and thermodynamics. The specific heat c of a substance may be defined by the equation

$$Q = mc(T_2 - T_1) \tag{3.155}$$

where Q is the amount of heat necessary to raise a mass m of the substance from temperature $T = T_1$ to temperature $T = T_2$. In the elementary definition of the specific heat in Eq. (3.155), c is regarded as a constant which is independent of temperature. This is not really true; c does in general depend on temperature, so

$$c = c(T) \tag{3.156}$$

In Exercise 2.21, it was found that the infinitesimal amount of heat dQ necessary to raise a mass m of a substance of specific heat $c(T)$ by an infinitesimal temperature dT was

$$dQ = mc(T)\,dT \tag{3.157}$$

Since the specific heat $c(T)$ depends on the temperature T, the infinitesimal amount of heat dQ depends on the temperature, and we write

$$dQ(T) = mc(T)\,dT \tag{3.158}$$

Eq. (3.158) says that the amount of heat $dQ(T)$ necessary to increase the temperature of a mass m by an amount dT is different at different temperatures.

Suppose the specific heat of a substance varies with temperature, as in Eq. (3.156). What is the *total* amount of heat Q necessary to increase the temperature of a mass m of the substance from T_1 to T_2? Suppose we construct a temperature axis, as shown in Fig. 3.11, and consider an infinitesimal temperature interval, of magnitude dT, located at temperature T. The infinitesimal amount of heat $dQ(T)$ necessary to increase the temperature of the substance by the infinitesimal amount dT is, from Eq. (3.158),

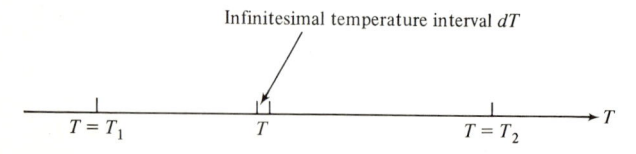

$$dQ(T) = mc(T)\,dT \tag{3.158}$$

Figure 3.11 Temperature axis, showing an infinitesimal temperature interval of magnitude dT located at a temperature T between the initial temperature T_1 and the final temperature T_2.

Then the *total* amount of heat Q necessary to raise the temperature from T_1 to T_2 is obtained by adding up or integrating all of the infinitesimal amounts of heat $dQ(T)$. We have

$$Q = \int dQ(T) \qquad (3.159)$$

where the variable of integration in Eq. (3.159) is the temperature T because $dQ(T)$ depends on T. Since $dQ(T)$ is given by Eq. (3.158), the expression for Q becomes

$$Q = \int mc(T)\, dT \qquad (3.160)$$

where, in Eq. (3.160), the variable of integration is still the temperature T because the specific heat $c(T)$ depends on T. Since the initial temperature of the substance is $T = T_1$ and the final temperature is $T = T_2$, these temperatures are the limits of integration in Eq. (3.160), which becomes

$$Q = m\int_{T_1}^{T_2} c(T)\, dT \qquad (3.161)$$

where the mass m is a constant independent of temperature and can be taken outside the integral. Eq. (3.161) gives the total amount of heat Q required to increase the temperature of a mass m of a substance, of temperature-dependent specific heat $c(T)$, from T_1 to T_2. To evaluate the definite integral in Eq. (3.161), one would have to know how the specific heat depends on the temperature, that is, to know the particular functional form of $c(T)$.

As a concrete calculation involving a temperature-dependent specific heat, we consider solid argon at very low temperatures. It is known that, below about 2 K, the specific heat of solid argon is proportional to T^3. Thus we have

$$c = c(T) = BT^3$$

where the constant B has the experimentally determined value $B = 6.26 \times 10^{-2}$ joule (kg)$^{-1}$ (K)$^{-4}$. Let's calculate the amount of heat Q required to increase the temperature of one kilogram of solid argon from 1 K to 2 K. From Eq. (3.161), the necessary amount of heat is

$$Q = m\int_{T_1}^{T_2} c(T)\, dT = m\int_1^2 BT^3\, dT = (6.26 \times 10^{-2})\int_1^2 T^3\, dT$$

on setting $m = 1$ kg and using $T_2 = 2$ K and $T_1 = 1$ K for the final and initial temperatures. Evaluating the integral yields

$$Q = (6.26 \times 10^{-2})\left[\frac{T^4}{4}\right]_1^2 = (6.26 \times 10^{-2})\left[\frac{16}{4} - \frac{1}{4}\right]\,\text{J}$$

106 CALCULUS FOR PHYSICS

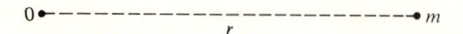

```
0●----------------------●m
           r
```

Figure 3.12 A point mass m located at a perpendicular distance r from an axis of rotation normal to the plane of the paper and passing through the point 0. The moment of inertia of the mass with respect to the axis of rotation is $I = mr^2$.

so our answer is $Q = 0.235$ joules for the amount of heat required to raise the temperature from 1 K to 2 K.

Note again how we have added up the infinitesimal amounts of heat $dQ(T)$ in Eq. (3.159) to find the total amount of heat Q. The process of adding up infinitesimal elements of some quantity by integrating is just what we did in the previous example of the work done by a variable force. The idea of using the definite integral as a sum of infinitesimal quantities (or differentials) was the same in both examples.

Our next example is from mechanics, and concerns the moment of inertia. The moment of inertia I of a *point* mass m located a distance r from an axis of rotation is

$$I = mr^2 \qquad (3.162)$$

Fig. 3.12 shows the mass m relative to an axis of rotation perpendicular to the plane of the paper and passing through the point 0. The moment of inertia I is the moment of inertia about this axis of rotation. If we have several point masses m_1, m_2, m_3 located at distances r_1, r_2, r_3 from the axis of rotation, we have the situation shown in Fig. 3.13. The moment of inertia I of this system of point masses, relative to an axis of rotation normal to the plane of the paper and passing through the point 0, is given by

$$I = m_1 r_1^2 + m_2 r_2^2 + m_3 r_3^2 \qquad (3.163)$$

Eq. (3.163) is an extension of the definition (3.162) to a number of point masses. We note that I is a *sum* of terms of the form mr^2.

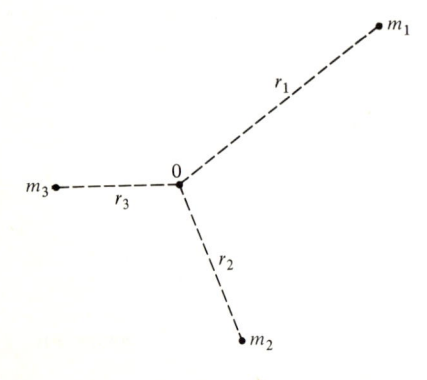

Figure 3.13 Three point masses m_1, m_2, m_3 at perpendicular distances r_1, r_2, r_3 from an axis of rotation normal to the plane of the paper and passing through the point 0. The moment of inertia with respect to the axis of rotation is $I = m_1 r_1^2 + m_2 r_2^2 + m_3 r_3^2$ and is a sum of terms of the form mr^2.

Given this definition of the moment of inertia, we would like to be able to calculate the moment of inertia of an *extended body*, rather than of a system of point masses. Examples of an extended body are a solid cylinder and a long thin rod. How do we calculate the moment of inertia of an extended body? Consider the homogeneous extended body of mass M and constant mass density ρ shown schematically in Fig. 3.14. We divide the body into infinitesimal elements of mass; the mass of each element is dm. We denote by r the perpendicular distance of an element dm from the axis shown. Each of the elements dm comprising the body is at a different distance r from the axis. Next, we construct products of the form

$$r^2 \, dm \tag{3.164}$$

for each element of mass dm. Noting that the expression (3.164) is the same as that in Eq. (3.162) for the moment of inertia I, we write

$$dI(r) = r^2 \, dm \tag{3.165}$$

where $dI(r)$ is the infinitesimal moment of inertia of the element of mass dm located at a distance r from the axis. We write $dI(r)$ to emphasize that the infinitesimal moment of inertia dI depends on the distance r. To calculate the moment of inertia I of the entire extended body, we add up all the infinitesimal moments of inertia $dI(r)$ by

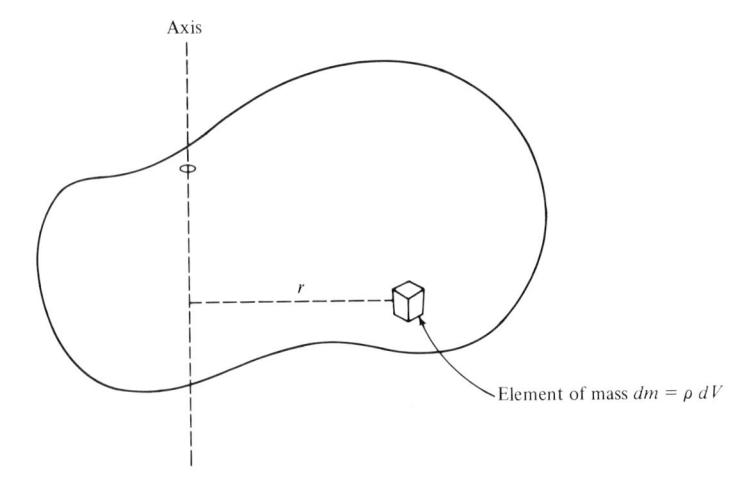

Figure 3.14 An extended body and its axis of rotation. The mass of the body is considered to be made up of infinitesimal elements of mass $dm = \rho \, dV$, where ρ is the constant mass density of the homogeneous body, and dV is an infinitesimal element of volume. The element of mass dm is located at a perpendicular distance r from the axis.

integration, and get

$$I = \int dI(r) = \int r^2 \, dm \qquad (3.166)$$

The variable of integration in Eq. (3.166) is r, the distance of an element of mass dm from the axis.

Next we must express the element of mass dm in terms of r, the variable of integration. We consider the volume V of the extended body in Fig. 3.14 to be divided up into infinitesimal elements of volume dV. The *shape* of the element of volume dV will be determined by what is convenient for the shape of the body. For a volume element dV of any shape, we have

$$dm = \rho \, dV \qquad (3.167)$$

because the body is homogeneous with a constant mass density ρ. In Eq. (3.167), the element of volume dV will depend in some way on the coordinate r and the dependence on r will be different for volume elements of different shapes. We emphasize the dependence of dV on r by rewriting Eq. (3.167) as

$$dm = \rho \, dV(r) \qquad (3.168)$$

Substituting Eq. (3.168) into Eq. (3.166) gives us

$$I = \int \rho \, r^2 \, dV(r) \qquad (3.169)$$

for the moment of inertia I and where the variable of integration in Eq. (3.169) is the coordinate r described above. The calculation of the moment of inertia using Eq. (3.169) becomes a question of using a convenient volume element dV for the shape of the body being considered. Keep in mind that, in calculating I using Eq. (3.166) or Eq. (3.169), we are again adding up, via integration, all of the infinitesimal elements dI to obtain the total moment of inertia.

Let's now use these results to calculate the moment of inertia I of a particular body. We will calculate I for a homogeneous solid right circular cylinder of height h, radius a, density ρ, and mass M, with respect to an axis passing through the center of the cylinder, as shown in Fig. 3.15. Our element of volume is a thin cylindrical shell (a hollow pipe) of height h and thickness dr located a distance r from the axis of the cylinder. The volume V of a right circular cylinder of radius r and height h is

$$V = \pi r^2 h \qquad (3.170)$$

The volume dV of the thin cylindrical shell is obtained by taking the differential of V given by Eq. (3.170) with respect to r. Thus

$$dV(r) = 2\pi h r \, dr \qquad (3.171)$$

SUMS AND INTEGRALS **109**

is the volume of the thin shell, which is also shown in Fig. 3.15. Then, from Eq. (3.168), the element of mass dm is

$$dm = 2\pi\rho h r\, dr \qquad (3.172)$$

and the integral in Eq. (3.166) for the moment of inertia I is

$$I = \int r^2\, dm \qquad (3.173)$$

$$I = 2\pi\rho h \int r^3\, dr \qquad (3.174)$$

The variable of integration in Eq. (3.174) is r, the distance from the cylinder axis to the cylindrical shell. The integral in Eq. (3.174) is essentially the "adding up" of all of the terms ($r^2\, dm$) for all of the shells comprising the cylinder. The distance r varies from $r = 0$ at the axis of the cylinder to $r = a$ at the surface of the cylinder. The limits in the integral in Eq. (3.174) are thus $r = 0$ and $r = a$, so Eq. (3.174) becomes

$$I = 2\pi\rho h \int_0^a r^3\, dr \qquad (3.175)$$

We evaluate the integral in Eq. (3.175) as

$$\int_0^a r^3\, dr = \left[\frac{r^4}{4}\right]_0^a = \frac{a^4}{4} \qquad (3.176)$$

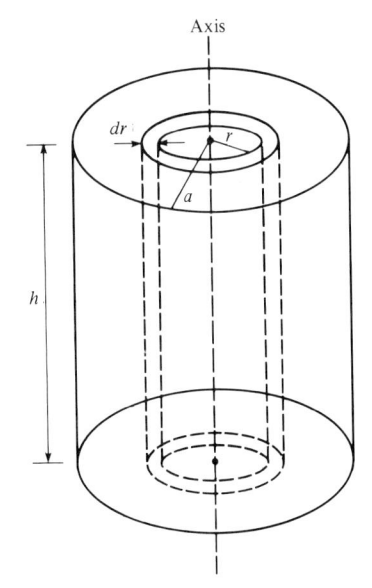

Figure 3.15 A solid right circular cylinder of height h and radius a, showing a volume element which is a thin cylindrical shell or pipe. The volume element, of height h and thickness dr, is located at a distance r from the axis of the cylinder. The element of mass $dm = \rho\, dV = 2\pi\rho h r\, dr$, where ρ is the constant mass density of the homogeneous cylinder.

so the moment of inertia becomes

$$I = (\pi \rho h a^4/2) = (\pi h a^2 \rho)\left(\frac{a^2}{2}\right) \qquad (3.177)$$

We note that $\pi h a^2$ is the volume of the cylinder of height h and radius a so $\pi h a^2 \rho$ is the mass M of the cylinder. Substituting this result into Eq. (3.177) gives

$$I = \frac{1}{2} M a^2 \qquad (3.178)$$

for the moment of inertia of the solid cylinder with respect to the axis shown in Fig. 3.15.

Note that once again we have used, in the integrals in Eqs. (3.166) and (3.169), the procedure of treating the integral as a sum of infinitesimal elements of the quantity of interest. (It should be pointed out, however, that certain subtle points apply to the calculation of the moments of inertia of some bodies of high symmetry, such as a sphere. A discussion of the physics involved is beyond the scope of this book. The interested reader is referred to, for example, *Berkeley Physics Course*, vol. 1: *Mechanics*.*

Our last example of the use of the definite integral as a sum of infinitesimal elements is from electricity, and concerns electrostatic potential. Consider a *point* electric charge of $+q$ coulombs (for convenience, we consider a positive charge) located at a point 0 as shown in Fig. 3.16. Consider also another point P located a distance r

Figure 3.16 A point charge $+q$ located a distance r from a point P.

from the charge q. Then it may be shown that the electrostatic potential V at the point P due to the charge q is

$$V = \frac{1}{4\pi\varepsilon_0} \frac{q}{r} \qquad (3.179)$$

In Eq. (3.179), the quantity ε_0 is a universal constant (called the permittivity of free space) and where we have *defined* the electrostatic potential V at point P as equal to zero when P is infinitely far from the charge. To emphasize the fact that the electrostatic potential V at the point P depends on the distance r from P to the point charge q, we

---

*C. Kittel, W. D. Knight, and M. A. Ruderman, *Berkeley Physics Course*, vol. 1: *Mechanics*, 1st ed., McGraw-Hill, New York, 1962, p. 243.

write
$$V(r) = \frac{1}{4\pi\varepsilon_0} \frac{q}{r} \quad (3.180)$$

The requirement that $V = 0$ when r is very large ($r \to \infty$) is fulfilled by the electrostatic potential function $V(r)$ in Eq. (3.180). If we have several point charges (also positive for convenience) q_1, q_2, q_3, located at different distances r_1, r_2, r_3 from a point P, then the electrostatic potential V at the point P is

$$V = \frac{1}{4\pi\varepsilon_0}\left[\frac{q_1}{r_1} + \frac{q_2}{r_2} + \frac{q_3}{r_3}\right] \quad (3.181)$$

where, again, the electrostatic potential is defined to be zero at a point P very distant from the charges.

The problem we want to address is the calculation of the electrostatic potential, at a point, due to a *continuous* distribution of electric charge, rather than a system of point charges. Examples of a continuous distribution of charge are a wire with a linear density of electric charge (in coulombs per meter) and a flat plate with a surface density of electric charge (in coulombs per square meter). Given some continuous distribution of electric charge, how do we calculate the electrostatic potential (at some point) due to that continuous charge distribution?

Our approach is to treat the continuous distribution of charge as an assembly of infinitesimal elements of charge, each of magnitude dq. Then we treat each infinitesimal element of charge dq as if it were a point charge. Suppose we have an infinitesimal element of charge dq located at a point 0, as shown in Fig. 3.17, and consider a point P a

```
    dq
 0 •----------------------• P
              r
```

Figure 3.17 An infinitesimal element of charge dq at a distance r from a point P. The electrostatic potential dV at point P due to the element of charge dq is $dV = (1/4\pi\varepsilon_0)(dq/r)$.

distance r from the element of charge. Then the electrostatic potential dV at point P due to the element of charge dq is

$$dV = \frac{1}{4\pi\varepsilon_0}\frac{dq}{r} \quad (3.182)$$

Note, in Eq. (3.182), the analogy to Eq. (3.179) for the electrostatic potential due to a point charge. In Eq. (3.182), we are treating the element of charge dq as if it were a point charge. We see from Eq. (3.182) that the infinitesimal element of electrostatic potential dV depends on the distance r; to emphasize this, we write

$$dV(r) = \frac{1}{4\pi\varepsilon_0}\frac{dq}{r} \quad (3.183)$$

112 CALCULUS FOR PHYSICS

(Incidentally, it is assumed that the universal use of the symbol V for both electrostatic potential and volume will not cause difficulty.)

Eq. (3.183) gives the element of electrostatic potential $dV(r)$ at a distance r from an element of charge dq. Suppose we have a continuous distribution of charge, like that indicated schematically in Fig. 3.18, and we want to calculate the electrostatic potential V at some point P. We treat the continuous distribution of charge as an assembly of infinitesimal elements of charge dq, each at a different distance r from the point P. Then the element of electrostatic potential at point P, due to the element of charge dq, is $dV(r)$ given by Eq. (3.183). The *total* electrostatic potential V at point P is obtained by adding up all of the elements $dV(r)$ by integration, so we have

$$V = \int dV(r) \qquad (3.184)$$

and

$$V = \frac{1}{4\pi\varepsilon_0} \int \frac{dq}{r} \qquad (3.185)$$

for the electrostatic potential V at point P. In the integrals in Eqs. (3.184) and (3.185), the variable of integration is r, the distance from the charge element dq to the point P.

Let's illustrate the calculation of the electrostatic potential due to a continuous distribution of charge. Fig. 3.19 shows a circular loop of

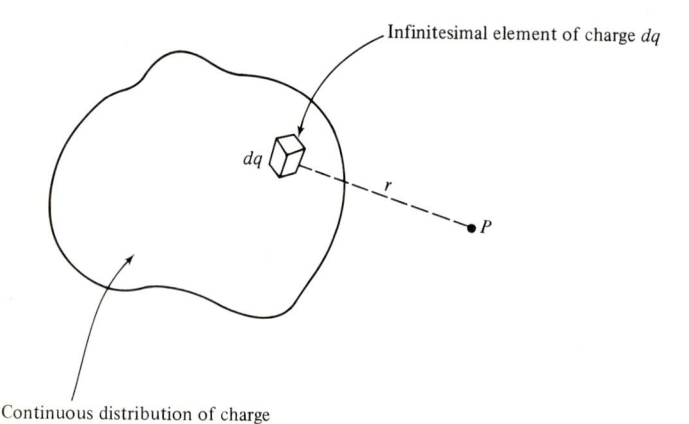

Figure 3.18 A continuous distribution of charge treated as an assembly of infinitesimal elements of charge dq. Each element dq is at a different distance r from the point P. The electrostatic potential $dV(r)$ at point P, due to the charge element dq, is $dV(r) = (1/4\pi\varepsilon_0)(dq/r)$.

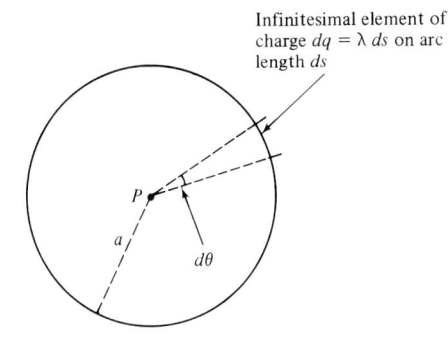

Figure 3.19 A circular wire loop of radius a. The element of charge $dq = \lambda\, ds$, where λ is the linear density of charge (in coulombs per meter) on the wire and ds is the element of arc length on the circumference of the circle. The infinitesimal angle $d\theta$ is subtended by ds.

wire, of radius a, on which is a linear distribution of charge of constant density λ coulombs per meter. We want to calculate the electrostatic potential V at the point P at the center of the circle. We let ds denote the element of arc length along the circumference of the circle, so the infinitesimal element of charge dq on the wire is

$$dq = \lambda\, ds \qquad (3.186)$$

where, dimensionally, we see that dq is in coulombs, λ is in coulombs per meter, and ds is in meters. To find the electrostatic potential V at the center of the circle, we add up all of the infinitesimal elements of potential dV given by Eq. (3.183). In this example of the circular loop,

$$dV = \frac{1}{4\pi\varepsilon_0} \frac{\lambda\, ds}{a} \qquad (3.187)$$

because each element of charge dq is at the same distance $r = a$ from the center of the circle. To find V, we integrate Eq. (3.187),

$$V = \int dV = \frac{\lambda}{4\pi\varepsilon_0 a} \int ds \qquad (3.188)$$

because λ, ε_0, and a are all constants. From Eq. (3.136), the element of arc length ds on a circle of radius a is

$$ds = a\, d\theta \qquad (3.189)$$

where $d\theta$ is the infinitesimal angle shown in Fig. 3.19. The integral in Eq. (3.188) is

$$\int ds = a \int_0^{2\pi} d\theta = 2\pi a \qquad (3.190)$$

where the limits of integration are as shown because, as discussed earlier, the angle θ varies between 0 and 2π in the circle. Substituting

114 CALCULUS FOR PHYSICS

Eq. (3.190) into Eq. (3.188) gives

$$V = \frac{\lambda}{2\varepsilon_0} \tag{3.191}$$

for the electrostatic potential V at the center of the circle. Note that V is, in this example, independent of the radius of the circle and depends only on the linear density of charge λ.

We conclude this section with a more complex calculation of the electrostatic potential due to a continuous distribution of charge. Consider, as shown in Fig. 3.20, a thin, flat circular disc of radius a, on one face of which is a constant surface density of charge of σ coulombs per square meter. We want to calculate the electrostatic potential V at a point P which is a perpendicular distance d from the disc and on a line through the center of the disc. We apply the same procedure that we used for the example of the circular loop. We find the infinitesimal element of electrostatic potential $dV(r)$ using Eq. (3.183) and then add up all the elements $dV(r)$ by integrating as in Eq. (3.184).

To calculate the element of charge dq, we see in Fig. 3.21 a top view of the disc shown in Fig. 3.20. We divide the area of the disc into circular rings of area dA, radius x, and thickness dx, where, from Eq. (2.173),

$$dA = 2\pi x \, dx \tag{3.192}$$

The element of charge on the disc is the charge dq contained on one of

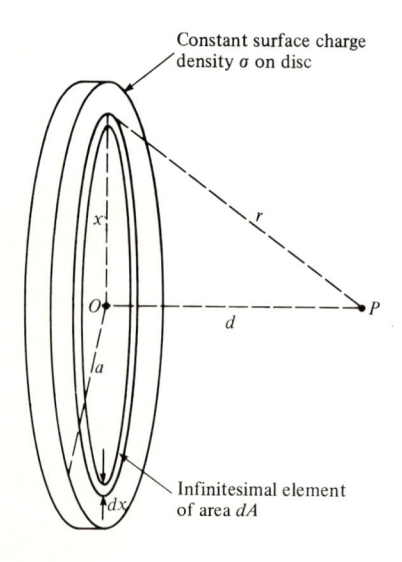

Figure 3.20 A flat circular disc of radius a on which is a constant density σ of surface charge (in coulombs per square meter). The point P is a distance d from the center O of the disc and OP is perpendicular to the plane of the disc. The element of area dA is a circular ring of radius x and width dx, where $dA = 2\pi x \, dx$. The ring of radius x is at a distance $r = (d^2 + x^2)^{1/2}$ from point P.

the circular rings of area dA into which we have divided the area of the disc. Since the surface density of charge is σ, the element of charge is

$$dq = \sigma\, dA = 2\pi\sigma x\, dx \qquad (3.193)$$

Eq. (3.193) gives the amount dq of charge on the circular ring of radius x and thickness dx.

Next, we have to find the distance r from each circular ring to the point P. Returning to Fig. 3.20, we see that all points on a circular ring of radius x are at the same distance r from point P, where

$$r^2 = d^2 + x^2 \qquad (3.194)$$

by the pythagorean theorem. Thus the distance r is given by

$$r = (d^2 + x^2)^{1/2} \qquad (3.195)$$

an equation giving the distance r in terms of the constant distance d and the radius x of the circular ring. Note from Eq. (3.195) that circular rings near the edge of the disc (those with larger values of x) are farther from point P than are rings near the center of the disc.

Since we now know dq from Eq. (3.193) and r from Eq. (3.195), we know the element dV of electrostatic potential at point P. Using Eq. (3.183), we have

$$dV(x) = \frac{1}{4\pi\varepsilon_0} \frac{2\pi\sigma x\, dx}{(d^2 + x^2)^{1/2}} \qquad (3.196)$$

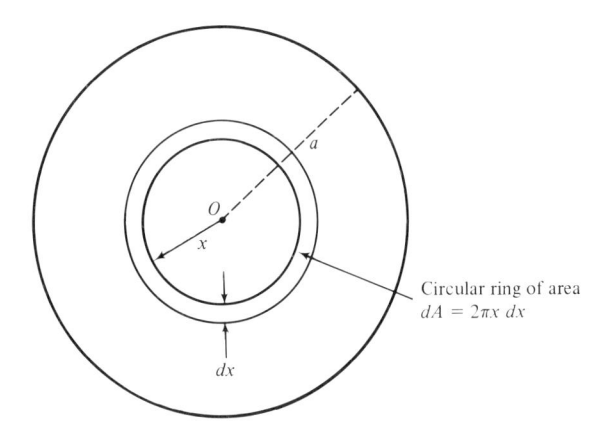

Figure 3.21 The flat circular disc with a surface charge density σ on it. The element of charge dq is the amount of charge on a circular ring of area $dA = 2\pi x\, dx$, so $dq = \sigma\, dA = 2\pi\sigma x\, dx$. (The drawing shows a top view of the disc.)

where we write $dV(x)$ to emphasize that the magnitude of the element dV of electrostatic potential at P depends on the radius x of the circular ring producing that element of potential. Simplifying Eq. (3.196), we have

$$dV(x) = \frac{\sigma}{2\varepsilon_0} \frac{x\,dx}{(d^2 + x^2)^{1/2}} \qquad (3.197)$$

Adding up all of the elements $dV(x)$ given by Eq. (3.197) by integrating, we get

$$V = \int dV(x) = \frac{\sigma}{2\varepsilon_0} \int \frac{x\,dx}{(d^2 + x^2)^{1/2}} \qquad (3.198)$$

for the total electrostatic potential V at point P due to all of the charge on the disc. The variable of integration x in Eq. (3.198) is the radius of the circular rings, so x varies from $x = 0$ (at the center of the disc) to $x = a$ at the rim of the disc of radius a. The limits of integration are thus $x = 0$ and $x = a$, and Eq. (3.198) becomes

$$V = \frac{\sigma}{2\varepsilon_0} \int_0^a \frac{x\,dx}{(d^2 + x^2)^{1/2}} \qquad (3.199)$$

To complete the problem, we evaluate the integral in Eq. (3.199) using the result found in Exercise 3.15 that

$$\int_0^a \frac{x\,dx}{(d^2 + x^2)^{1/2}} = \left[(d^2 + x^2)^{1/2}\right]_0^a = (d^2 + a^2)^{1/2} - (d^2)^{1/2}$$

$$(3.200)$$

Substituting Eq. (3.200) into Eq. (3.199) gives the final result

$$V = \frac{\sigma}{2\varepsilon_0}\left[(d^2 + a^2)^{1/2} - d\right] \qquad (3.201)$$

for the electrostatic potential V at a distance d from the center of a circular disc, of radius a, bearing a surface charge density of σ coulombs per square meter. We note that, reasonably, V depends on d, a, and σ.

At the risk of verbal overkill, let me reiterate that, once again, all of the problems in this section were done in the same basic way. We found the infinitesimal element of the quantity of interest, whether it was work, heat, moment of inertia, or electrostatic potential. Then we added up all of the infinitesimal elements to get the total amount of the quantity of interest. This method is constantly used in physics and is also applied to vector quantities as well as the scalar quantities we have used in our examples.

Exercises

3.21 Calculate the moment of inertia of a hollow circularly cylindrical "pipe" of outer radius R_2, inner radius R_1, length L, mass M, and whose solid portion has a constant mass density ρ. The axis is through the center of the cylinder, parallel to its length.

3.22 Given a circular loop of wire of radius a bearing a linear charge density of λ coulombs per meter. Consider a point P that is a perpendicular distance d from the plane of the loop and on a line passing through the center of the loop. Calculate the electrostatic potential at point P due to the charge on the wire loop.

AVERAGE VALUE OF A FUNCTION

As our last topic in the application of the definite integral to physics, we consider the *average value* of a function. If we have a continuous function $f(x)$ over the interval $a \leq x \leq b$, then the average value of f, denoted by $\bar{f}$, with respect to x, is defined as

$$\bar{f} = \frac{1}{b-a} \int_a^b f(x)\, dx \qquad (3.202)$$

That the definition in Eq. (3.202) of the average value $\bar{f}$ is plausible may be seen in a casual way as follows. We divide the x axis between $x = a$ and $x = b$ into n intervals of infinitesimal (very small) length dx, where

$$n = \frac{b-a}{dx} \qquad (3.203)$$

Then the average value $\bar{f}$ may be thought of, roughly, as the sum of the n values of the function $f(x)$ in each of n intervals dx, divided by n. If we "sum" the function $f(x)$ by integration and divide by n as given by Eq. (3.203), we obtain the expression for $\bar{f}$ in the definition given in Eq. (3.202).

It is important in calculating the average value of a function to keep in mind the interval of the independent variable being considered. For example, consider the function

$$f(t) = \sin^2 \omega t \qquad (3.204)$$

where t is the time and ω is a constant. Let us calculate $\bar{f}$ over the time interval from $t = 0$ to $t = (2\pi/\omega)$ s. We note that the period of the sine function is 2π rad, so the function $\sin \omega t$ has a period or "repeat time" of $(2\pi/\omega)$ s. We are thus finding the average value of $\sin^2 \omega t$

118 CALCULUS FOR PHYSICS

over a time interval of one period. We have from Eq. (3.202) that

$$\overline{\sin^2\omega t} = \frac{1}{(2\pi/\omega)} \int_0^{2\pi/\omega} \sin^2\omega t \, dt = \frac{1}{2} \qquad (3.205)$$

where the bar over $\sin^2\omega t$ indicates its average value. Our result is thus that the average value of $\sin^2\omega t$ over the interval $0 \le t \le (2\pi/\omega)$ is $1/2$.

Exercises

3.23 Calculate the average value of $\cos^2\omega t$ over the interval $0 \le t \le (2\pi/\omega)$.

APPENDIX

REVIEW OF SOME TRIGONOMETRIC RELATIONS

We review here some useful trigonometric relations. For more detail, I suggest pages 78–88 of *Tables of Integrals and Other Mathematical Data* by H. B. Dwight, 4th ed., Macmillan, New York, 1961.

Given the right triangle ABC, shown in Fig. A.1, whose sides are of lengths a, b, and c, respectively. The angle θ is the angle BAC as shown. Then the basic trigonometric functions of the angle θ are defined as follows:

$$\text{sine } \theta = \sin \theta = a/c \quad \text{(A.1)}$$

$$\text{cosine } \theta = \cos \theta = b/c \quad \text{(A.2)}$$

$$\text{tangent } \theta = \tan \theta = a/b \quad \text{(A.3)}$$

$$\text{cotangent } \theta = \cot \theta = b/a \quad \text{(A.4)}$$

$$\text{secant } \theta = \sec \theta = c/b = (1/\cos \theta) \quad \text{(A.5)}$$

$$\text{cosecant } \theta = \csc \theta = c/a = (1/\sin \theta) \quad \text{(A.6)}$$

These trigonometric functions are used extensively in physics. From

120 CALCULUS FOR PHYSICS

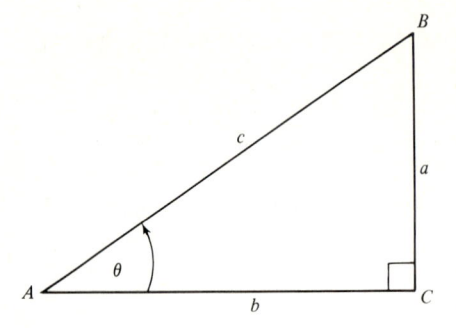

Figure A.1 Right triangle used to define the trigonometric functions.

(A.1)–(A.3), it follows also that

$$a = c \sin \theta \tag{A.7}$$
$$b = c \cos \theta \tag{A.8}$$

so, if c and θ are known, the lengths a and b are determined.

The following *trigonometric identities* are true for any values of the angles θ and ϕ; we use the notation $\sin^2\theta \equiv (\sin\theta)^2$, and so forth.

$$\sin^2\theta + \cos^2\theta = 1 \tag{A.9}$$
$$\sin(\theta + \phi) = \sin\theta\cos\phi + \cos\theta\sin\phi \tag{A.10}$$
$$\cos(\theta + \phi) = \cos\theta\cos\phi - \sin\theta\sin\phi \tag{A.11}$$
$$\sin(\theta - \phi) = \sin\theta\cos\phi - \cos\theta\sin\phi \tag{A.12}$$
$$\cos(\theta - \phi) = \cos\theta\cos\phi + \sin\theta\sin\phi \tag{A.13}$$
$$\sin\theta + \sin\phi = 2\sin\tfrac{1}{2}(\theta + \phi)\cos\tfrac{1}{2}(\theta - \phi) \tag{A.14}$$
$$\sin\theta - \sin\phi = 2\sin\tfrac{1}{2}(\theta - \phi)\cos\tfrac{1}{2}(\theta + \phi) \tag{A.15}$$
$$\cos\theta + \cos\phi = 2\cos\tfrac{1}{2}(\theta + \phi)\sin\tfrac{1}{2}(\theta - \phi) \tag{A.16}$$
$$\cos\theta - \cos\phi = 2\sin\tfrac{1}{2}(\theta + \phi)\cos\tfrac{1}{2}(\theta - \phi) \tag{A.17}$$
$$\sin 2\theta = 2\sin\theta\cos\theta \tag{A.18}$$
$$\cos 2\theta = 2\cos^2\theta - 1 \tag{A.19}$$

As an example of the utility of these trigonometric identities, consider the following. Suppose we know $\sin A$, where A is some angle (less than 90°). What is the value of the sine of the angle $(180° - A)$, that is, $\sin(180° - A)$? Using (A.12) with $\theta = 180°$, $\phi = A$, we have

$$\sin(180° - A) = \sin 180° \cos A - \cos 180° \sin A \tag{A.20}$$

REVIEW OF SOME TRIGONOMETRIC RELATIONS 121

Recalling that $\sin 180° = \sin 0° = 0$, and $\cos 180° = -1$, we obtain

$$\sin(180° - A) = (0)(\cos A) - (-1)(\sin A) = \sin A \quad (A.21)$$

showing that $\sin(180° - A) = \sin A$. Thus, for example, $\sin 162° = \sin(180° - 18°) = \sin 18° = 0.309$.

We should also mention the *inverse* trigonometric functions. If

$$y = \sin x \quad (A.22)$$

an equation that says that y is the sine of the angle x, we may solve (A.22) for x in terms of y, writing

$$x = \sin^{-1} y \quad (A.23)$$

an equation that is read "x is the angle whose sine is y." As an example,

$$0.707 = \sin 45° \quad (A.24)$$

$$45° = \sin^{-1}(0.707) \quad (A.25)$$

Note that x in (A.23) is a many-valued function of y; more than one value of x corresponds to a single value of y. For example, in addition to (A.25), it is also true that

$$135° = \sin^{-1}(0.707) \quad (A.26)$$

There are also other inverse trigonometric functions. If

$$y = \cos x \quad (A.27)$$

then its inverse is

$$x = \cos^{-1} y \quad (A.28)$$

and if

$$y = \tan x \quad (A.29)$$

its inverse is

$$x = \tan^{-1} y \quad (A.30)$$

Another notation is also used for inverse trigonometric functions, namely

$$x = \arcsin y \equiv \sin^{-1} y \quad (A.31)$$

Both notations in (A.31) mean the same thing, namely "x is the angle whose sine is y."

SOLUTIONS TO EXERCISES

1.1 Since the expression $w = 7u^2 + 6u + 3$ gives w as a function of u, w is the dependent variable and u is the independent variable. Thus, assigning a value to u (for example, $u = 2$) determines the value of w. If $u = 2$, $w = 43$.

1.2 We can solve Eq. (1.1), $y = x^2$, for x in terms of y, obtaining

$$x = \pm\sqrt{y}$$

In this relation, the dependent variable x is a function of the independent variable y. Note that x is a many (i.e., two)-valued function of y since two values of the dependent variable x correspond to each value of the independent variable y.

1.3 The functional relation between C and r is $C = 2\pi r$. In this relation, C is the dependent variable and r is the independent variable.

1.4 Since $f(x) = 3x^2 + 2$, we have
(a) $f(2) = 3 \cdot (2)^2 + 2 = 12 + 2 = 14$;
(b) $f(0) = 3 \cdot (0)^2 + 2 = 0 + 2 = 2$;
(c) $f(-1) = 3 \cdot (-1)^2 + 2 = 3 + 2 = 5$.

1.5 Since $y(x, t) = A\sin(kx - \omega t)$, where A, k, and ω are constants, the dependent variable y is a function of the *two* independent variables x and t. Then (a) $y(0,0)$ is obtained by substituting $x = 0$, $t = 0$ in the expression for $y(x, t)$, giving

$$y(0,0) = A\sin(k \cdot 0 - \omega \cdot 0) = A\sin(0) = 0$$

(b) $y(0, t)$ is obtained by setting $x = 0$, giving

$$y(0, t) = A\sin(k \cdot 0 - \omega t) = A\sin(0 - \omega t) = A\sin(-\omega t) = -A\sin\omega t,$$

so $y(0, t)$ is itself a function of the variable t and is not just a number as was $y(0,0) = 0$ in part a above; (c) $y(x, 0)$ is obtained by setting $t = 0$, giving

$$y(x,0) = A \sin(kx - \omega \cdot 0) = A \sin(kx - 0) = A \sin kx$$

1.6 If we replace the variable x in $f(x)$ by the new variable $(x - a)$, we get $f(x - a)$. Since in this problem

$$f(x) = (1 - x^2)^{1/2}$$

$$f(x - a) = \left(1 - [x - a]^2\right)^{1/2} = \left(1 - [x^2 - 2ax + a^2]\right)^{1/2}$$

so

$$f(x - a) = (1 - x^2 + 2ax - a^2)^{1/2}$$

1.7 (a) $f(x) = x - 2x^2$

x	0	0.05	0.10	0.15	0.20	0.25	0.30	0.35	0.40	0.45	0.50
$f(x)$	0	.045	.080	0.105	.120	0.125	0.120	.105	.080	.045	0

(b) The curve is shown in Fig. S.1.

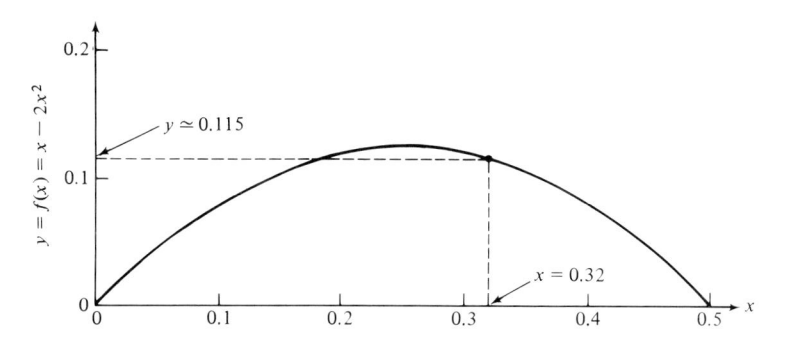

Figure S.1 Graph of $f(x) = x - 2x^2$ for $0 \leq x \leq 0.5$.

(c) This curve is a parabola whose axis is parallel to the y axis; (d) From the curve, $y \cong 0.115$ when $x = 0.32$; (e) From the curve, $y = 0$ when $x = 0$ and also when $x = 0.5$, in agreement with setting $y = 0$ in the equation

$$y = x - 2x^2$$

If $y = 0$, we have

$$0 = x - 2x^2$$
$$0 = x(1 - 2x)$$

leading to the solutions $x = 0$ and $x = (1/2) = 0.5$.

1.8 (a) Since the equation of a straight line of slope m and y intercept $(0, b)$ is given by Eq. (1.39) as $y = mx + b$, $m = 2$ since the slope is given as equal to 2. Since the line passes through the origin $(0,0)$, its y intercept is zero, so $b = 0$. Thus the equation of the

124 CALCULUS FOR PHYSICS

required straight line is $y = 2x$; Since the slope $m = \tan\theta$, where θ is the angle made by the line with the x axis,

$$\tan\theta = 2$$
$$\theta = \tan^{-1} 2$$
$$\theta = 63.4° = 1.11 \text{ radians}$$

(c) The graph is shown in Fig. S.2.

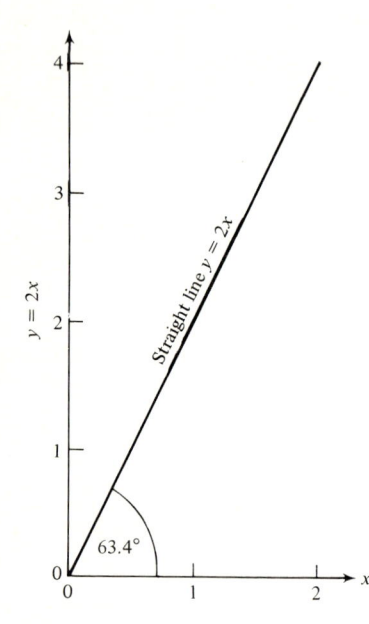

Figure S.2 Graph of $y = f(x) = 2x$ for $0 \le x \le 2$.

1.9 (a) We begin by calculating a table of values of

$$y = f(x - a) = \left[1 - (x - a)^2\right]^{1/2}$$

for the value $a = 0$ of the constant a. If $a = 0$, the function f becomes

$$y = f(x - 0) = f(x) = (1 - x^2)^{1/2}$$

We use, as requested, values of x from $x = 1$ to $x = -1$ in intervals of 0.2; we consider only positive values of y:

x	1.0	0.8	0.6	0.4	0.2	0	−0.2	−0.4	−0.6	−0.8	−1.0
y	0	0.6	0.8	0.92	0.98	1	0.98	0.92	0.8	0.6	0

The graph of $y = f(x - a)$ for $a = 0$ is shown in Fig. S.3.

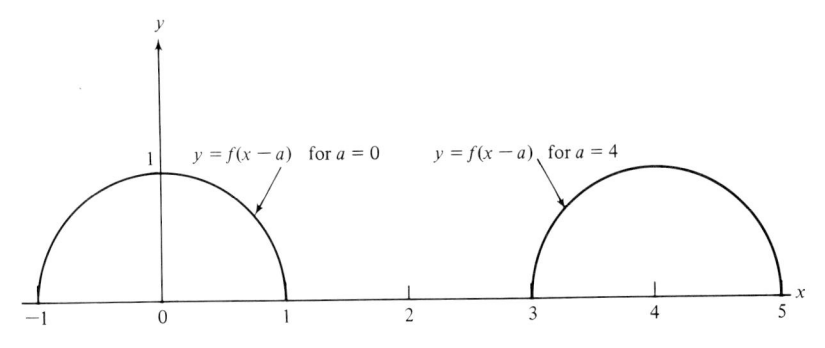

Figure S.3 Graph of $y = f(x - a) = [1 - (x - a)^2]^{1/2}$ for $a = 0$ and for $a = 4$.

(b) We now repeat the graphing procedure for $a = 4$. If $a = 4$, then the function $f(x - a)$ is

$$y = f(x - 4) = \left[1 - (x - 4)^2\right]^{1/2}$$

We make the table, as requested, for values of x between 3 and 5, at intervals of 0.2; again considering only positive values of y:

x	3.0	3.2	3.4	3.6	3.8	4.0	4.2	4.4	4.6	4.8	5.0
y	0	0.6	0.8	0.92	0.98	1	0.98	0.92	0.8	0.6	0

The graph of $f(x - a)$ for $a = 4$ is also shown in Fig. S.3. Considering the graph of $f(x - a)$ for $a = 0$, we see that the graph of

$$y = f(x - a) = (1 - x^2)^{1/2}$$

is a semicircle with its center at $x = 0$. Similarly, for $a = 4$, the graph of

$$y = f(x - a) = \left[1 - (x - 4)^2\right]^{1/2}$$

is a semicircle with its center at $x = 4$. More generally, the graph of

$$f(x - a) = \left[1 - (x - a)^2\right]^{1/2}$$

is a semicircle with its center at $x = a$ since we are considering only positive values of y.

1.10 Since 2π radians = 360°, π radians = 180°, and we have
(a) $(\pi/8)$ radians = $(180/8)° = 22.5°$;
(b) $(3\pi/4)$ radians = $(3 \cdot 180/4)° = 135°$;
(c) 3π radians = $(3 \cdot 180)° = 540°$;
(d) $(31\pi/32)$ radians = $(31 \cdot 180/32)° = 174.38°$.

126 CALCULUS FOR PHYSICS

1.11 We calculate the values of cos x for $0 \leq x \leq 4\pi$ in multiples of $(\pi/8)$ radians:
(a)

x	0	$\pi/8$	$2\pi/8$	$3\pi/8$	$4\pi/8$	$5\pi/8$	$6\pi/8$	$7\pi/8$
cos x	1	0.924	0.707	0.383	0	−0.383	−0.707	−0.924

x	$8\pi/8$	$9\pi/8$	$10\pi/8$	$11\pi/8$	$12\pi/8$	$13\pi/8$	$14\pi/8$	$15\pi/8$	$16\pi/8$
cos x	−1	−0.924	−0.707	−0.383	0	0.383	0.707	0.924	1

x	$17\pi/8$	$18\pi/8$	$19\pi/8$	$20\pi/8$	$21\pi/8$	$22\pi/8$	$23\pi/8$
cos x	0.924	0.707	0.383	0	−0.383	−0.707	−0.924

x	$24\pi/8$	$25\pi/8$	$26\pi/8$	$27\pi/8$	$28\pi/8$	$29\pi/8$	$30\pi/8$	$31\pi/8$	$32\pi/8$
cos x	−1	−0.924	−0.707	−0.383	0	0.383	0.707	0.924	1

(b) We make the graph of cos x as a function of x shown in Fig. S.4; each interval on the x axis is equal to $(\pi/8)$ radians.

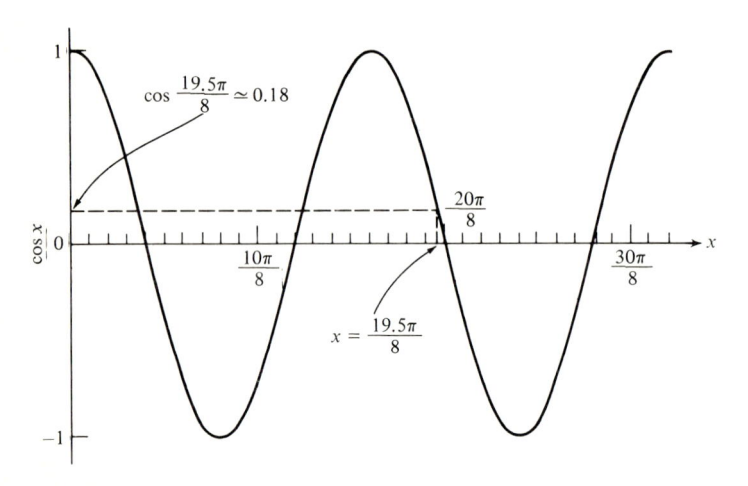

Figure S.4 Graph of cos x as a function of x for $0 \leq x \leq (32\pi/8)$. Each interval on the x axis is $(\pi/8)$ radians.

(c) From the graph, the maximum value of cos x is 1; the minimum value is −1; (d) We can see from the graph that the function cos x repeats itself (i.e., goes from 1 to −1 and back to 1) when x goes from zero to $(16\pi/8)$ radians. Hence cos x *is* periodic, with period $(16\pi/8)$ radians = 2π radians; (e) The period is 2π radians; (f) There are 2 cycles of cos x on the graph. The first cycle is for values of x between $x = 0$ and $x = (16\pi/8)$; the second is for values of x between $x = (16\pi/8)$ and $x = (32\pi/8)$ radians; (g) The cosine of $(39\pi/16)$ radians = $\cos(19.5\pi/8)$. From the graph $\cos(19.5\pi/8) \cong 0.18$. The precise value is 0.195.

2.1 Since $f(x) = x^3$, we have

$$f(x + \Delta x) = (x + \Delta x)^3 = x^3 + 3x^2(\Delta x) + 3x(\Delta x)^2 + (\Delta x)^3$$

$$f(x + \Delta x) - f(x) = 3x^2(\Delta x) + 3x(\Delta x)^2 + (\Delta x)^3$$

$$[f(x + \Delta x) - f(x)]/(\Delta x) = 3x^2 + 3x(\Delta x) + (\Delta x)^2$$

Taking the limit as $\Delta x \to 0$ gives us

$$f'(x) = \lim_{\Delta x \to 0} \left[3x^2 + 3x(\Delta x) + (\Delta x)^2\right] = 3x^2$$

so the derivative of $f(x) = x^3$ is $f'(x) = 3x^2$.

2.2 Since $f(x) = (1/x)$, we have $f(x + \Delta x) = [1/(x + \Delta x)]$ and thus

$$f(x + \Delta x) - f(x) = \frac{1}{x + \Delta x} - \frac{1}{x} = \frac{x - (x + \Delta x)}{x(x + \Delta x)} = \frac{-\Delta x}{x(x + \Delta x)}$$

Then

$$\frac{f(x + \Delta x) - f(x)}{\Delta x} = \frac{1}{\Delta x}\left(\frac{-\Delta x}{x(x + \Delta x)}\right) = \frac{-1}{x(x + \Delta x)}$$

Taking the limit as $\Delta x \to 0$ gives us

$$f'(x) = \lim_{\Delta x \to 0}\left[\frac{-1}{x(x + \Delta x)}\right] = \frac{-1}{x(x)} = \frac{-1}{x^2}$$

so the derivative of $f(x) = (1/x)$ is $f'(x) = -1/(x^2)$.

2.3 Using the product rule in Eq. (2.40) with $u(x) = e^x$ and $v(x) = \sin x$, we have

$$\frac{d}{dx}[e^x \sin x] = e^x \frac{d}{dx}(\sin x) + (\sin x)\frac{d}{dx}(e^x)$$

$$= e^x \cos x + (\sin x) e^x$$

$$= e^x(\sin x + \cos x)$$

2.4 Using the quotient rule in Eq. (2.42) with $u(x) = \cos x$ and $v(x) = \sin x$, we have

$$\frac{d}{dx}\left[\frac{\cos x}{\sin x}\right] = \frac{1}{\sin^2 x}\left[(\sin x)\frac{d}{dx}(\cos x) - (\cos x)\frac{d}{dx}(\sin x)\right]$$

$$= \frac{1}{\sin^2 x}[(\sin x)(-\sin x) - (\cos x)(\cos x)]$$

$$= \frac{-(\sin^2 x + \cos^2 x)}{\sin^2 x} = \frac{-1}{\sin^2 x} = -\csc^2 x$$

so we have shown that

$$\frac{d}{dx}[\cot x] = -\csc^2 x$$

2.5 To calculate the derivative of x^3, we see that x^3 is x^n with $n = 3$, so Eq. (2.35) becomes

$$\frac{d}{dx}[x^3] = 3x^{3-1} = 3x^2$$

128 CALCULUS FOR PHYSICS

To differentiate $(1/x) = x^{-1}$, we have $n = -1$, so Eq. (2.35) is

$$\frac{d}{dx}[x^{-1}] = (-1)x^{-1-1} = -x^{-2} = \frac{-1}{x^2}$$

These results are the same as those obtained in Exercises 2.1 and 2.2.

2.6 Since $y(x) = e^{-2x^2}$, we have $y(x) = g(u) = e^u$ and $u(x) = -2x^2$ so, by the chain rule, either in the form (2.67) or the form (2.49), we have

$$y'(x) = g'(u)u'(x) = (e^u)(-4x) = (-4x)e^{-2x^2}$$

2.7 Using the chain rule again, we have $y(x) = u^4 = g(u)$ and $u(x) = (x^2 + 3x - 2)$ so

$$y'(x) = g'(u)u'(x) = (4u^3)(2x + 3) = 4(x^2 + 3x - 2)^3(2x + 3)$$

2.8 In this problem, we will have to use the chain rule twice. First

$$y(x) = g(u) = \sin u; u(x) = e^{x^2}$$

$$y'(x) = g'(u)u'(x) = (\cos u)u'(x) = \left[\cos(e^{x^2})\right]u'(x) \quad (1)$$

Next, we have to find the derivative $u'(x)$, where

$$u'(x) = \frac{d}{dx}[e^{x^2}]$$

by using the chain rule. Just as in Exercise 2.6 above, we say that

$$u(x) = g(v) = e^v; v(x) = x^2$$

$$u'(x) = g'(v)v'(x) = (e^v)(2x) = 2xe^{x^2} \quad (2)$$

Combining the results (1) and (2) above, we obtain

$$y'(x) = \left[\cos(e^{x^2})\right](2xe^{x^2})$$

so our final answer is

$$y'(x) = \frac{d}{dx}\left[\sin(e^{x^2})\right] = 2xe^{x^2}\cos(e^{x^2})$$

2.9 From Exercise 2.3 above, we had the result that, for the function $f(x) = e^x \sin x$, the derivative $f'(x)$ is

$$f'(x) = e^x(\cos x + \sin x)$$

To find $f''(x)$, we differentiate $f'(x)$, obtaining

$$f''(x) = \frac{d}{dx}[f'(x)] = \frac{d}{dx}[e^x(\cos x + \sin x)]$$

$$= e^x \frac{d}{dx}(\cos x + \sin x) + (\cos x + \sin x)\frac{d}{dx}(e^x)$$

$$= e^x(-\sin x + \cos x) + (\cos x + \sin x)(e^x)$$

$$= -e^x \sin x + e^x \cos x + e^x \cos x + e^x \sin x$$

$$= e^x \cos x + e^x \cos x = 2e^x \cos x$$

$$f''(x) = 2e^x \cos x$$

SOLUTIONS TO EXERCISES 129

2.10 Since $y = f(x) = 6x + 2$, and $x_1 = 1.00$, $(x_1 + \Delta x) = 1.01$, $\Delta x = 0.01$, we have

$$f(x_1) = f(1) = 6(1) + 2 = 8.00$$

$$f(x_1 + \Delta x) = f(1.01) = 6(1.01) + 2 = 8.06$$

(a) $\Delta y = f(x_1 + \Delta x) - f(x_1) = 8.06 - 8.00 = 0.06$

$\dfrac{\Delta y}{\Delta x} = \dfrac{0.06}{0.01} = 6 = $ average rate of change of y with respect to x for x between 1.00 and 1.01

(b) Since $\Delta y = 6(\Delta x)$, $\Delta y = 6(0.01) = 0.06$ when $\Delta x = 0.01$. The change Δy in y is $\Delta y = 0.06$ when x changes from 1.00 to 1.01.

2.11 We are given that $f(x) = x^3$, so (a) $f'(x) = 3x^2$ is the instantaneous rate of change of x^3 with respect to x; (b) when $x = 1$, $f'(1) = 3(1)^2 = 3$ is the value of the rate of change.

2.12 (a) Since s is directly proportional to t, with constant of proportionality B, the equation giving s as a function of t is $s = Bt^3$; (b) The rate of change of s with respect to time t is

$$\frac{ds}{dt} = \frac{d}{dt}[Bt^3] = 3Bt^2$$

(c) Since velocity v is the rate of change of distance with respect to time,

$$v = \frac{ds}{dt} = 3Bt^2$$

giving the velocity v as a function of time.

2.13 (a) Since $s = 2.4t^2$, the rate of change of distance s with respect to time is

$$\frac{ds}{dt} = 4.8t$$

(b) Yes, (ds/dt) does vary with (is directly proportional to) time. (c) Velocity v is the rate of change of distance with respect to time, so

$$v = \frac{ds}{dt} = 4.8t$$

When $t = 1$ second (that is, 1 second after the block begins to move), $v = 4.8(1) = 4.8$ meters per second.

2.14 (a) Since $C = 2\pi r$, the rate of change of C with respect to r is given by

$$\frac{dC}{dr} = \frac{d}{dr}[2\pi r] = 2\pi$$

where (dC/dr) is the rate of change of C with respect to r; (b) This rate of change is the change in the circumference C (in meters) per meter of change in the radius r. The rate of change (dC/dr) is equal to 2π, meaning that C changes by 2π ($= 6.28$) meters for a change of 1 meter in r. Note that, in this case, the rate of change (dC/dr) does *not* depend on the value of the radius r.

2.15 We found in part c of Exercise 2.12 that the velocity $v = 3Bt^2$. Since the acceleration is the rate of change (dv/dt) of the velocity with respect to time, we have

$$a = \frac{dv}{dt} = \frac{d}{dt}[3Bt^2] = 6Bt$$

since B is a constant. This acceleration a is *not* constant with time (as it is for a vertically falling body without air resistance).

130 CALCULUS FOR PHYSICS

2.16 Using the notation employed in the text, let
$$y = g(u) = 6 \cos u$$
$$u = f(x) = 6x^4$$
Then
$$\frac{dy}{dx} = \left(\frac{dy}{du}\right)\left(\frac{du}{dx}\right) = (-6 \sin u)(24x^3)$$
$$\frac{dy}{dx} = (-144x^3)\sin(6x^4)$$
Multiplying both sides of this equation by the differential dx gives
$$dy = [(-144x^3)\sin(6x^4)] \, dx$$
for the required differential dy.

2.17 Since $A = \pi r^2$, we can take the differential dA as
$$dA = \pi(2r) \, dr = (2\pi) r \, dr$$
where dr is the differential of r. Dividing both sides of the expression for dA by dt, the differential of time t, gives
$$\frac{dA}{dt} = (2\pi) r \frac{dr}{dt}$$
This equation says that the rate of change (dA/dt) of the area with respect to time equals the constant 2π times the radius r times (dr/dt), the rate of change of the radius with respect to time. Note that the rate of change (dA/dt) depends on *both* r and (dr/dt).

2.18 Since distance dx equals the rate v times the time dt, we have $dx = v \, dt$. This equation says that the particle moves the infinitesimal distance dx in the infinitesimal time dt while traveling at the constant velocity v.

2.19 (a) Since $a = (dv/dt)$, we can multiply both sides of this equation by the differential dt, obtaining
$$a \, dt = \left(\frac{dv}{dt}\right) dt = dv$$
so our result is
$$dv = a \, dt$$

(b) The meaning of our result is as follows. If a particle or body moves with constant acceleration a for the infinitesimal length of time dt, its velocity v will change by the very small amount dv.

2.20 Using $dy = f'(x) \, dx = (3x^2) \, dx$ with $dx = 0.00001$, we evaluate $f'(x) = 3x^2$ for $x = 2.000005$, so we have
$$f'(2.000005) = 3(2.000005)^2 = 3(4.00002) = 12.00006 \cong 12$$
so
$$dy \cong (12)(0.00001) = 0.00012.$$

2.21 (a) From the information given,
$$dQ = mc \, dT$$

giving dQ in terms of m, c, and dT, where dQ is the infinitesimal amount of heat necessary to raise the temperature of the mass m by a very small amount dT; (b) Dividing both sides of the equation for dQ by dT gives

$$mc = \frac{dQ}{dT} \quad \text{or} \quad c = \frac{1}{m}\frac{dQ}{dT}$$

as the equation defining the specific heat c.

2.22 (a) Since $f(x) = x^2 + 2$, $f'(x) = 2x$, and $f'(5) = 10$, so $\tan\theta = 10$ is the slope of the geometric tangent at $x = 5$; (b) The angle θ, where $\tan\theta = 10$, is the angle the geometric tangent makes with the x axis. Then $\theta = \tan^{-1}10 = 84.3°$; (c) The slope of the curve at any point is the slope of the geometric tangent at that point. At $x = 2$, the slope of the geometric tangent, and hence of the curve, is $f'(2) = 2(2) = 4$.

2.23 (a) The graph is shown in Fig. S.5. The values of s and t are calculated from $s = 2t^3$.

s	0	.002	.016	.054	.128	.250	.432	.686	1.024	1.458	2.000	2.662
t	0	0.1	0.2	0.3	0.4	0.5	0.6	0.7	0.8	0.9	1.0	1.1

s	3.456	4.394	5.488	6.750	8.192	9.826	11.664	13.718	16.000
t	1.2	1.3	1.4	1.5	1.6	1.7	1.8	1.9	2.0

where s is in meters and t is in seconds; (b) The slope is given by (ds/dt) evaluated at $t = 1$ second, so

$$\text{Slope} = \left(\frac{ds}{dt}\right)_{t=1} = (6t^2)_{t=1} = 6 \text{ meters per second}$$

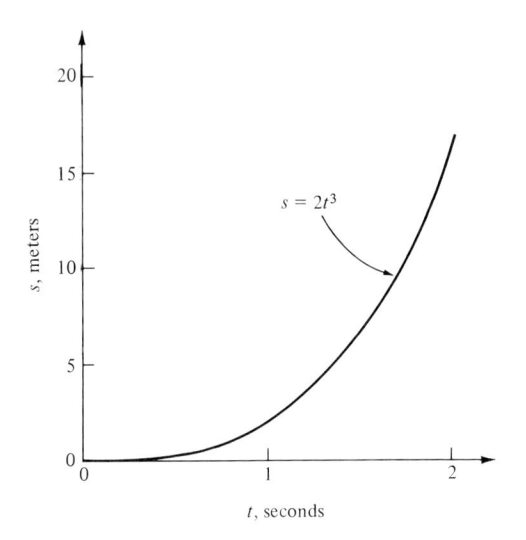

Figure S.5 Graph of $s = 2t^3$ for $0 \leq t \leq 2$ seconds.

132 CALCULUS FOR PHYSICS

(c) The velocity v is the time rate of change of distance, so

$$v = \frac{ds}{dt} = 6t^2$$

From this equation, we calculate values of v and t as follows:

v	0	0.06	0.24	0.54	0.96	1.50	2.16	2.94	3.84	4.86
t	0	0.1	0.2	0.3	0.4	0.5	0.6	0.7	0.8	0.9

v	6.00	7.26	8.64	10.14	11.76	13.50
t	1.0	1.1	1.2	1.3	1.4	1.5

v	15.36	17.34	19.44	21.66	24.00
t	1.6	1.7	1.8	1.9	2.0

The values of v are in meters per second and t is in seconds. The graph of v as a function of t is shown in Fig. S.6. This curve is a parabola whose equation is $v = 6t^2$; (d) The

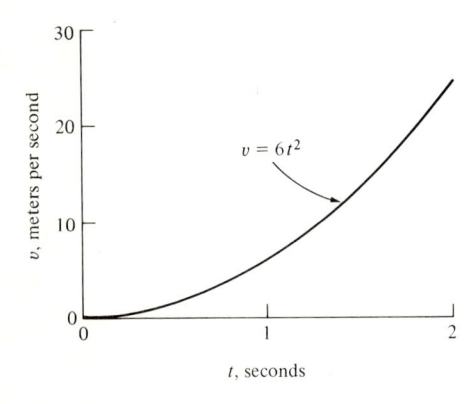

Figure S.6 Graph of $v = 6t^2$ for $0 \leq t \leq 2$ seconds.

slope of the curve $v = 6t^2$ is given by the derivative (dv/dt) where

$$\frac{dv}{dt} = 12t$$

When $t = 1$ second,

$$\text{Slope} = \left(\frac{dv}{dt}\right)_{t=1} = (12t)_{t=1} = 12 \text{ (meters per second) per second}$$

(e) The acceleration a is the rate of change of velocity with respect to time so

$$a = \frac{dv}{dt} = 12t$$

The graph of a as a function of t is shown in Fig. S.7.

SOLUTIONS TO EXERCISES 133

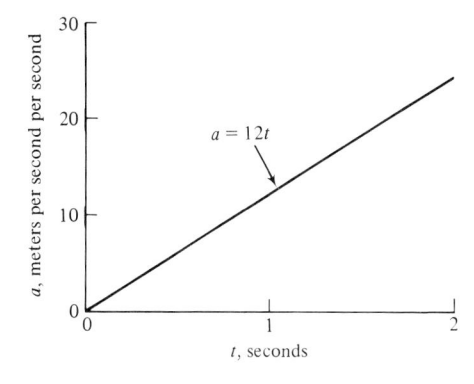

Figure S.7 Graph of $a = 12t$ for $0 \leq t \leq 2$ seconds.

This "curve" is the straight line whose equation is $a = 12t$; (f) The acceleration a is *not* constant. From the graph in part e, we see that $a = 12t$ increases linearly with increasing time.

2.24 (a) To find the value of x at which $\sin x$ has its first maximum, we first find the first derivative $f'(x)$ and set it equal to zero. Thus

$$f'(x) = \frac{d}{dx}(\sin x) = \cos x = 0$$

For what values of x does $\cos x = 0$? The values are the critical points

$$x = \frac{\pi}{2} = 90°; \; x = \frac{3\pi}{2} = 270°, \ldots$$

Thus $f(x) = \sin x$ has its first critical point at $x = (\pi/2)$ radians. Since we know from the graph of $\sin x$ that (for $x \geq 0$), $\sin x$ *increases* as x increases from zero, the first critical point $x = (\pi/2)$ is a maximum; (b) In the same way, we see that the first minimum in $\sin x$ is at the second critical point $x = (3\pi/2)$ radians; (c) To check, we apply the second derivative test, where

$$f''(x) = \frac{d}{dx}(\cos x) = -\sin x$$

When $x = (\pi/2)$, $f''(\pi/2) = -\sin(\pi/2) = -1$ so the second derivative is *negative* at the critical point $x = (\pi/2)$, meaning this is a *maximum*. When $x = (3\pi/2)$,

$$f''\left(\frac{3\pi}{2}\right) = -\sin\left(\frac{3\pi}{2}\right) = -(-1) = +1$$

so the second derivative is *positive* at the critical point $x = (3\pi/2)$, meaning this is a *minimum*.

2.25 (a) Since the vertical height y is given by

$$y = (v_0 \sin \theta)t - 4.9t^2$$

we want to find the value of t for which y is a maximum. We take the derivative (dy/dt) and set it equal to zero:

$$\frac{dy}{dt} = (v_0 \sin \theta) - 9.8t = 0$$

134 CALCULUS FOR PHYSICS

where we keep in mind that v_0 and θ are constants which are fixed permanently at the initial instant of time $t = 0$. Solving for t, we get

$$t = \frac{v_0 \sin \theta}{9.8}$$

as the time at which y is a maximum. (We know we are dealing with a maximum value of y, and not a minimum, from the physics of the situation; that is, y increases as the ball moves, y reaches a maximum, and then y decreases until the ball hits the ground.) If we knew the particular values of v_0 and θ, we could calculate the value of t explicitly. The equation for t above holds for all values of v_0 and θ; (b) We want to know the horizontal distance x moved by the ball when the vertical height y is a maximum, so we want to know x when $t = (v_0 \sin \theta / 9.8)$ seconds. Since x is given as a function of time by

$$x = (v_0 \cos \theta) t$$

we simply substitute $t = (v_0 \sin \theta / 9.8)$ into the expression for x as a function of t, obtaining

$$x = (v_0 \cos \theta) \left(\frac{v_0 \sin \theta}{9.8} \right) = \frac{v_0^2 \sin \theta \cos \theta}{9.8}$$

This is the value of x when y is a maximum.

3.1 Use the substitution $u = 3x$, so $du = 3\,dx$, and the integral becomes

$$\frac{1}{3} \int \cos u \, du = \frac{1}{3} (\sin u) = \frac{1}{3} \sin 3x$$

so our answer is

$$\int \cos 3x \, dx = \frac{1}{3} \sin 3x + C$$

3.2 Use the substitution $u = (x - a)$, so $du = dx$ and the integral becomes

$$\int u^2 \, du = \frac{1}{3} u^3 = \frac{1}{3} (x - a)^3$$

and our answer is

$$\int (x - a)^2 \, dx = \frac{1}{3} (x - a)^3 + C$$

3.3 Use the substitution $u = x^2$, so $du = 2x \, dx$, $(1/2) \, du = x \, dx$ and the integral becomes

$$\frac{1}{2} \int e^{-u} \, du = \frac{-1}{2} e^{-u} = \frac{-1}{2} e^{-x^2}$$

so our answer is

$$\int x e^{-x^2} \, dx = \frac{-1}{2} e^{-x^2} + C$$

3.4 Use $u = x$, $dv = \cos x \, dx$, so $du = dx$ and

$$v = \int dv = \int \cos x \, dx = \sin x + C'$$

$$uv = x(\sin x + C') = x \sin x + C'x$$

and

$$\int u\,dv = \int x\cos x\,dx = uv - \int v\,du$$

$$= x\sin x + C'x - \int(\sin x + C')\,dx$$

$$= x\sin x + C'x + \int(-\sin x)\,dx - \int C'\,dx$$

$$= x\sin x + C'x + \cos x - C'x = x\sin x + \cos x$$

(Note that the constant C' drops out and could have been ignored from the start.) Our answer is therefore

$$\int x\cos x\,dx = x\sin x + \cos x + C$$

3.5 Use $u = x$, $du = dx$, $dv = e^x\,dx$, so $v = \int dv = \int e^x\,dx = e^x$, where, just as in 3.4 above, we ignore any constant of integration in the integration of dv to get v. Then

$$\int xe^x\,dx = \int u\,dv = uv - \int v\,du = xe^x - \int e^x\,dx = xe^x - e^x$$

and our final answer is

$$\int xe^x\,dx = xe^x - e^x + C = (x-1)e^x + C$$

3.6 The velocity v is the rate of change of distance s with respect to time, so

$$v = \frac{ds}{dt} = V$$

where V is a constant. Multiplying by the differential dt gives $ds = V\,dt$. To get s we integrate over the variable t, obtaining

$$s = \int ds = \int V\,dt = V\int dt = Vt + C$$

so

$$s(t) = Vt + C$$

To determine the constant C, we know that $s = 100$ when $t = 0$, so $s(0) = 100$. Putting $t = 0$ in the equation for $s(t)$ gives $s(0) = C$, so the constant $C = 100$ meters, and the complete equation for the distance $s(t)$ as a function of time is

$$s(t) = Vt + 100 \text{ meters}$$

where s is in meters when t is in seconds.

3.7 Since $(dy/dx) = 6 - 2x$ we have $dy = (6 - 2x)\,dx$ so

$$y = \int dy = \int(6 - 2x)\,dx = 6x - x^2 + C$$

$$y(x) = 6x - x^2 + C$$

Since $y = 9$ when $x = 3$, we have

$$9 = 6(3) - (3)^2 + C = 18 - 9 + C$$

$$C = 0$$

136 CALCULUS FOR PHYSICS

In this case the constant of integration has the value zero, and the function $y(x)$ is

$$y(x) = 6x - x^2$$

This function is the parabola shown in Fig. 2.17.

3.8 Again we are given the value of the acceleration, which is constant with the value zero. Then, if v is the velocity and setting $A = 0$ in Eq. (3.55), we get

$$\frac{dv}{dt} = 0$$

so

$$dv = 0 \cdot dt$$

$$v = \int dv = \int 0 \cdot dt$$

What is the integral of zero, or, in other words, what function has zero as its derivative? The answer is that a constant has zero as its derivative, so we have for the velocity

$$v(t) = C$$

where C is a constant. The initial condition given in the problem is that $v = 100$ meters per second when $t = 0$, so

$$v(0) = 100 \text{ meters per second}$$

Since $v(t) = C$, meaning that the velocity is *constant* and does not change with time, it is also true that

$$v(0) = C$$

so the value of the constant C is $C = 100$ meters per second. The complete equation for $v(t)$ is therefore

$$v(t) = 100 \text{ meters per second}$$

an equation which says that the velocity is constant with the value 100 meters per second (and thus the acceleration is zero because the velocity is not changing with time). Note that this equation tells us how v behaves with time in that it tells us that v is *independent* of time.

3.9 (a) $x_1^2 + x_2^2 + x_3^2 + x_4^2 = \sum_{i=1}^{4} x_i^2$

(b) $1 + y + y^2 + y^3 + y^4 + y^5 = \sum_{i=0}^{5} y^i$ (since $y^0 = 1$)

(c) $1^2 + 2^2 + 3^2 = \sum_{k=1}^{3} k^2$

3.10 Here the function $F(x) = \int \sin x \, dx = -\cos x$, so

$$\int_0^{\pi} \sin x \, dx = [-\cos x]_0^{\pi} = -[\cos \pi - \cos 0] = -[-1 - 1] = 2$$

3.11 In this problem the function $F(x)$ is given by

$$F(x) = \int x^2 \, dx = (1/3)x^3$$

so
$$\int_0^2 x^2\,dx = \left[\frac{1}{3}x^3\right]_0^2 = \frac{1}{3}[2^3 - 0^3] = \frac{8}{3}$$

3.12 Here the function $F(x)$ is given by $F(x) = \int e^{-x}\,dx = -e^{-x}$, so

$$\int_0^\infty e^{-x}\,dx = [-e^{-x}]_0^\infty = -\left[\frac{1}{e^x}\right]_0^\infty = -\left[\frac{1}{e^\infty} - \frac{1}{e^0}\right] = -\left[\frac{1}{\infty} - 1\right] = 1$$

3.13 Here the function $F(x) = \int(x-a)^2\,dx$, which was found in Exercise 3.2 to be

$$\int(x-a)^2\,dx = \frac{1}{3}(x-a)^3$$

so

$$\int_0^a (x-a)^2\,dx = \left[\frac{1}{3}(x-a)^3\right]_0^a = \frac{1}{3}\left[(a-a)^3 - (0-a)^3\right] = \frac{1}{3}a^3$$

3.14 In this case the function $F(x)$ is $F(x) = \int x^{-2}\,dx = -x^{-1}$, so

$$\int_\infty^b x^{-2}\,dx = -\left[\frac{1}{x}\right]_\infty^b = -\left[\frac{1}{b} - \frac{1}{\infty}\right] = -\frac{1}{b}$$

3.15 In this example, the function

$$F(x) = \int \frac{x\,dx}{(d^2 + x^2)^{1/2}}$$

We make the substitution $(d^2 + x^2) = u$, so $du = 2x\,dx$, $x\,dx = (1/2)\,du$, and the integral becomes

$$\int \frac{x\,dx}{(d^2 + x^2)} = \frac{1}{2}\int \frac{du}{u^{1/2}} = \frac{1}{2}(2u^{1/2}) = u^{1/2} = (d^2 + x^2)^{1/2}$$

Then the definite integral is

$$\int_0^a \frac{x\,dx}{(d^2 + x^2)^{1/2}} = \left[(d^2 + x^2)^{1/2}\right]_0^a = (d^2 + a^2)^{1/2} - d$$

3.16 The area A between the curve $f(x) = 2x + 1$ and the x axis between $x = 1$ and $x = 2$ is

$$A = \int_1^2 (2x+1)\,dx = [x^2 + x]_1^2 = [2^2 + 2 - 1^2 - 1] = 4$$

3.17 In Eq. (3.107),

$$A \equiv \int_a^b f(x)\,dx = \text{area between } f(x) \text{ and } x \text{ axis between } x = a \text{ and } x = b$$

$$A_1 \equiv \int_a^c f(x)\,dx = \text{area between } f(x) \text{ and } x \text{ axis between } x = a \text{ and } x = c$$

$$A_2 \equiv \int_c^b f(x)\,dx = \text{area between } f(x) \text{ and } x \text{ axis between } x = c \text{ and } x = b$$

Hence Eq. (3.107) says that area A = area A_1 + area A_2.

138 CALCULUS FOR PHYSICS

3.18 Since $p = p(V) = CV^{-1}$, the area A is

$$A = \int_{V_1}^{V_2} p(V)\, dV = \int_{V_1}^{V_2} \frac{C}{V}\, dV = C\int_{V_1}^{V_2} \frac{dV}{V}$$

$$A = C[\ln V]_{V_1}^{V_2} = C[\ln V_2 - \ln V_1] = C\ln\left(\frac{V_2}{V_1}\right)$$

Since $V_2 > V_1$, $(V_2/V_1) > 1$, $\ln(V_2/V_1) > 0$, and $A > 0$.

3.19 Fig. S.8 shows the x axis with the interval $a \leq x \leq b$. Also shown is an element of length dx located at a point x. We want to calculate L, the distance from $x = a$ to

Element of length dx

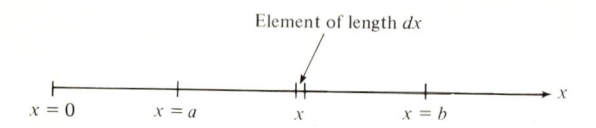

|———————+————++————+————————→ x
$x=0$ $x=a$ x $x=b$

Figure S.8 The x axis, showing an element of length dx located at the point x between $x = a$ and $x = b$.

$x = b$. We find L by adding up (integrating) all the elements of length dx between $x = a$ and $x = b$, so we have

$$L = \int dx = \int_a^b dx$$

Here the variable of integration is x and the lower and upper limits of the integral are a and b, respectively. Then

$$L = \int_a^b dx = [x]_a^b = (b - a)$$

the answer we would have expected from the results of analytic geometry.

3.20 Fig. S.9 shows the straight line $f(x) = x$ and the shaded strip is an element of area dA, where $dA = x\, dx$ since the width of the strip is dx and its height is $f(x) = x$. Note that the area $dA = x\, dx$ depends on x. The total area A is obtained by integrating all of the elements dA, so

$$A = \int dA = \int_0^a x\, dx = \left[\frac{x^2}{2}\right]_0^a = \left(\frac{a^2}{2} - 0\right) = \frac{a^2}{2}$$

where the variable of integration is x and x varies from $x = 0$ to $x = a$ so those are the limits of the definite integral.

3.21 The top view of the pipe is shown in Fig. S.10. The volume element dV is a thin cylindrical shell a distance r from the axis, which is normal to the plane of the paper and passes through the center O of the pipe. Then $dV = 2\pi Lr\, dr$ because L is the length of the pipe (the height of the cylinder). The element of mass dm is $dm = \rho\, dV = 2\pi \rho Lr\, dr$. The moment of inertia

$$I = \int r^2\, dm = 2\pi \rho L \int_{R_1}^{R_2} r^3\, dr = 2\pi \rho L \left[\frac{r^4}{4}\right]_{R_1}^{R_2}$$

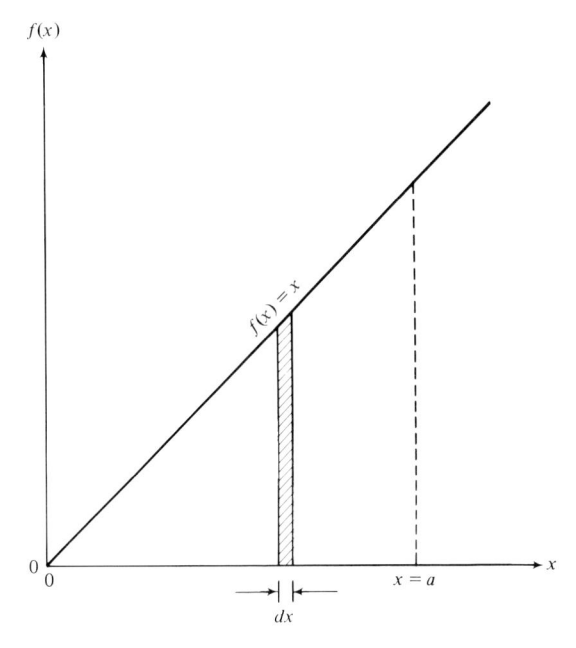

Figure S.9 Graph of $f(x) = x$ for $0 \le x \le a$, showing a strip (shaded) of width dx and area $dA = x\,dx$.

because the variable of integration r varies from $r = R_1$ to $r = R_2$. Then

$$I = (\pi \rho L/2)(R_2^4 - R_1^4) = (\pi \rho L/2)(R_2^2 + R_1^2)(R_2^2 - R_1^2)$$

Note that $\pi L(R_2^2 - R_1^2)$ is the volume of the solid part of the pipe, so $\pi \rho L(R_2^2 - R_1^2) = M$, the mass of the pipe. Thus

$$I = \frac{1}{2}M(R_1^2 + R_2^2)$$

is the required moment of inertia.

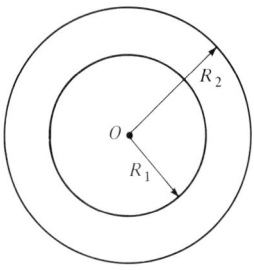

Figure S.10 End view of a hollow circularly cylindrical "pipe" of inner radius R_1 and outer radius R_2.

140 CALCULUS FOR PHYSICS

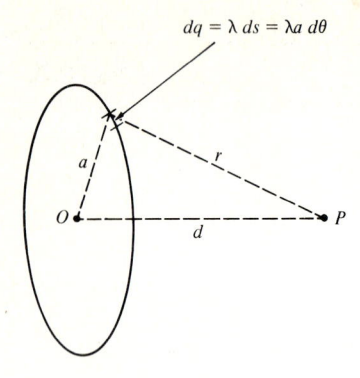

Figure S.11 Circular loop of radius a, showing an element of charge dq located a distance r from point P. The point P is a perpendicular distance d from the center O of the circle.

3.22 The geometry is as shown in Fig. S.11. The distance r from the element of charge dq to point P is $r = (a^2 + d^2)^{1/2}$. The charge element $dq = \lambda\, ds = \lambda a\, d\theta$ on using Eq. (3.189). The element of electrostatic potential at point P due to the element of charge dq is

$$dV = \frac{1}{4\pi\varepsilon_0}\frac{dq}{r} = \frac{1}{4\pi\varepsilon_0}\frac{\lambda a\, d\theta}{(a^2+d^2)^{1/2}}$$

where λ, a, d are all constants. The total electrostatic potential at point p is

$$V = \int dV = \frac{1}{4\pi\varepsilon_0}\frac{\lambda a}{(a^2+d^2)^{1/2}}\int d\theta$$

where the variable of integration θ varies from $\theta = 0$ to $\theta = 2\pi$ on going around the circular loop. Then

$$V = \frac{1}{4\pi\varepsilon_0}\frac{\lambda a}{(a^2+d^2)^{1/2}}\int_0^{2\pi} d\theta = \frac{2\pi\lambda a}{4\pi\varepsilon_0(a^2+d^2)^{1/2}} = \frac{\lambda a}{2\varepsilon_0(a^2+d^2)^{1/2}}$$

so V depends on λ, a, and d. Note that, if $d \to 0$, we get $V = (\lambda/2\varepsilon_0)$, in agreement with our previous result in Eq. (3.191) for the electrostatic potential at the center 0 of the circular loop.

3.23 To evaluate $\int \cos^2 \omega t\, dt$ we substitute $u = \omega t$, $du = \omega\, dt$, so

$$\int \cos^2 \omega t\, dt = \frac{1}{\omega}\int \cos^2 u\, du = \frac{1}{\omega}\left[\frac{u}{2} + \frac{\sin 2u}{4}\right] = \frac{1}{\omega}\left[\frac{\omega t}{2} + \frac{\sin 2\omega t}{4}\right]$$

on using a table of integrals. Then

$$\frac{1}{2\pi/\omega}\int_0^{2\pi/\omega}\cos^2\omega t\, dt = \frac{\omega}{2\pi}\frac{1}{\omega}\left[\frac{\omega t}{2} + \frac{\sin 2\omega t}{4}\right]_0^{2\pi/\omega}$$

$$= \frac{1}{2\pi}\left[\frac{2\pi}{2} + \frac{\sin 4\pi}{4}\right] = \frac{1}{2}$$

INDEX

Acceleration:
 graph as function of time, 65
 motion with constant, 46,
  62–66, 78–80
 as rate of change of velocity,
  45–46
 and second derivative, 45–47
 as second derivative of distance,
  46
 in simple harmonic motion, 47
 as slope of graph of velocity as
  function of time, 65
Air resistance, 46, 68
Angle:
 element of, 98
 made by geometric tangent with
  x axis, 60–61
 made by straight line with
  x axis, 11
 subtended by arc of circle, 13
Antiderivative, 71–72
Antidifferentiation, 73
Approximation, small angle,
 14–15

Arc length of circle, 12, 13, 97
 element of, 98
 integration of, 99–100
Area:
 of circular ring, 55, 114
 under curve of function, 92,
  94–95
 differential, 55
 element of, 94–95
 integration of, 94–96
 on surface of circular disc,
  115–116
Average rate of change (see Rate
 of change, average)
Average value of a function,
 117–118
Axis of rotation, 106, 107, 109,
 110

Chain rule, 26–29
 and differential, 49–50
 notation, 27, 29
Change in function, 56–57

141

142 INDEX

Charge, electric (*see* Electric charge)
Circle:
  arc length of, 12, 13, 97
  circumference of, 13, 97–99
    calculation of, by integration, 97–99
  equation of, 15
  parametric equations, 16
Circular disc, charged, 114
Circular loop, charged, 112
Circular ring, 55, 114
Concave graph, 67
Condition, initial (*see* Initial condition)
Constant:
  arbitrary, in integral, 73
  definition of, 1
  derivative of, 23
  of integration: definition of, 73
    for independent variable other than time, 83
    and initial condition, 80, 81, 84
Cos x (*see* Cosine function)
Cosine function (cos x):
  cycle, 126
  derivative, 25
  differential, 51
  graph, 126
  integral, 75
  period, 126
Critical point:
  definition of, 67
  derivatives at, 67
Curve:
  area under, 92, 94–95
  geometric tangent to, 60–61
  slope of, 59–60, 62
  (*See also* Graph)
Cylinder:
  hollow, moment of inertia, 117 (Exercise 3.21)

Cylinder (*Cont.*):
  homogeneous, moment of inertia, 108–110
Cylindrical shell, 108–109

Definite integral (*see* Integral, definite)
Density:
  of electric charge: linear, 113
    surface, 114
  mass, 108
Derivative:
  calculation of, 23–26
  chain rule, 26–29
  connection of, with rate of change, 34–38
  of constant, 23
  of cosine function, 25
  at critical point, 67
  definition of, 18–22
    example of use of, 20
  of exponential function, 25
  of function of a function, 26–29
  geometric applications, 58–62
    physical uses, 62–66
    summary, 65–66
  nomenclature, 21–22
  notation, 21–22, 40–41
  operation, 23
  of power of variable, 24–25
  of product, 25
  of quotient, 25
  as ratio of differentials, 48–49
  with respect to time, 39
  second (*see* Second derivative)
  of sine function, 25
  of sum, 24
  of tangent function, 25–26
  third, 30
Differential:
  applications of: to change in function, 56–57

INDEX **143**

Differential, applications
   of (*Cont.*):
  to geometry, 55–56
  to physics, 52–58
  "cancellation," 49
  and chain rule, 49–50
  of cosine function, 51
  cube of, 56
  definition of, 47–48
  of exponential function, 51
  in finding rates of change, 50–51
  of function, 48
  of independent variable, 48
  integration of, 72
  of logarithmic function, 51
  notation, 47–48, 51
  operation of taking, 51
  of power of variable, 51
  of product, 51
  relation of, to derivative, 48–49
  of sine function, 51
  as small quantity, 52–53, 94–96, 102–106
  square of, 55
  of sum, 51
Differential area, 55
Differential distance, 53
Differential quantity, 53
Differential volume, 56
Differentiation,
  definition of, 21
  inverse of, 72
  operation of, 23
Distance:
  differential, 53
  graph as function of time, 62–64
  integration over, 102–103
  meaning of, in physics problems, 38–39
  projectile in two dimensions, 70 (Exercise 2.25)
  vertically thrown projectile, 69

Dummy index, 85
Dummy variable, 89

Electric charge:
  circular loop of, 112–114
  continuous distribution, 111
  element of, 111
    on element of arc length on circle, 113
    on element of area on circular disc, 115
  linear density of, 113
  point, 110
  surface density of, 114
Electrostatic potential:
  due to circular loop of charge, 112–114
  due to continuous distribution of charge, 111–116
  due to point charge, 110
  due to several point charges, 111
  due to surface charge on circular disc, 114–116
  element of, 111–112
    due to element of linear charge, 112–113
    due to element of surface charge, 115–116
  zero of, 110–111
Element:
  of angle, 98
  of arc length (circle), 98
    integration of, 99–100
  of area, 94–95
    integrating, 94–96
    on surface of circular disc, 115–116
  of electric charge, 111
  of electrostatic potential, 111–112

Element, of electrostatic
   potential (*Cont.*):
     due to element of electric
       charge, 111
     due to element of linear
       electric charge on circular
       loop, 111–112
     due to element of surface
       electric charge on circular
       disc, 115–116
   of heat, 52–53, 104–106
     integration of, 104–106
   of internal energy, 52–53
   of length, 53, 94, 102
   of linear electric charge on
     circular loop, 113
   of mass, 107–110
   of moment of inertia, 107, 108
     integration of, 108–110
   of surface electric charge on
     circular disc, 115
   of time, 54
   of volume, 108
   of work, 54, 101–102
     integration of, 102–103
Equation:
   circle, 15
   parabola, 10
   parametric, 16–17
   straight line, 10
Exponential function, 25
   derivative, 25
   differential, 51
   integral, 75
   notation, 76

Falling body:
   acceleration of, 46, 62–66
   under gravity, 46, 62–66
Force:
   constant, 53–54, 101
   proportional to position, 103

Force (*Cont.*):
   variable, 101–103
   work done by, 53–54, 101–103
Function(s):
   area under curve, 92, 94–95
   average value of, 117–118
   change in, when independent
     variable changes, 56–57
   definition of, 2
   derivative of, 18–20
   differential of, 48
   domain of, 2
   of a function, 4
     derivative of, 26–29
   graph of, 8–11
   inverse, 22
   inverse trigonometric, 121
   many-valued, 2
   maxima and minima of, 66–69
   of one variable, 2, 5
   product of (*see* Product of
     functions)
   range of, 2
   of several variables, 5–6
   single-valued, 2
   sum of (*see* Sum, of functions)
   of time, 38
   trigonometric (*see*
     Trigonometric functions)
   value at a point, 6–8
     read from graph, 10
   well-behaved, 18–19
Functional relationship, 2

Gradient, temperature, 44
Graph:
   of acceleration as function
     of time, 65
   area under, 92, 94–95
   concave downward, 67
   concave upward, 67
   of cosine function, 126

Graph (*Cont.*):
  of distance as function of time,
    62–64
    velocity as slope of, 63–64
  of function, 8–11
  geometric tangent to, 60–61
  intercept of (*see* Intercept of
    graph)
  of parabola, 9
  slope of, 59–60, 62
  of straight line, 11
  of trigonometric functions,
    12–15
  of velocity as function of time,
    64–65, 82–83
    acceleration as slope of, 65,
      82
    initial velocity as intercept
      of, 82–83
Gravity, acceleration under, 46

Heat:
  element of, 52–53, 104–106
    integration of, 104–106
  necessary to produce tem-
    perature increase, 104–106
  specific (*see* Specific heat)

Identities, trigonometric, 120–121
Increment of variable, 19, 32–33
Independent variable, 2–3,
  differential of, 48
Independent variables, 5
Index:
  dummy, 85
  in summation notation, 84
Inertia, moment of (*see* Moment
  of inertia)
Infinitesimal amount of work, 54
Infinitesimal distance, 53–54
Infinitesimal element (*see*
  Element)
Infinitesimal length, 54
Infinitesimal moment of inertia,
  107, 108
  integration of, 108–110
Infinitesimal quantity, 53
Infinitesimal time, 54
Initial condition:
  and constant of integration,
    80, 81, 84
  definition of, 80
  for independent variable other
    than time, 83
  more than one, 81–82
  on velocity, 80
Integral:
  as antiderivative, 72
  of cosine function, 75
  definite: as area under curve,
    89–93
    definition of, 85–87
    elementary properties, 89
    evaluation, 87–89
    fundamental theorem, 87–88
    geometric interpretation,
      89–93
    interchange of limits, 89
    as limit of sum, 87, 92
    limits, 87
    notation, 87, 88
    replacing sum, 96
    as sum of infinitesimals,
      94–96, 99–100
  elementary properties, 74–75
  of exponential function, 75
  indefinite, 73
  of power of variable, 75
  replacing sum, 96
  of sine function, 75
  of sum, 74
Integrand, 72
Integration:
  of acceleration, 79
  and antiderivative, 72

Integration (*Cont.*):
  constant of, 73
    (*See also* Constant, of integration)
  of differential, 72
  by parts, 76–78
  by substitution, 75–76
  techniques of, 75–78
  variable of, 74
    physical meanings, 103
Intercept of graph:
  of straight line, 10
  of velocity as function of time, 82–83
Internal energy, 52–53

Length, element of, 53, 94, 102
Line, straight (*see* Straight line)
Ln x (*see* Logarithm function)
Logarithm function (ln x):
  derivative, 26
  differential, 51

Mass, element of, 107–110
Mass density, 108
Maximum of a function:
  definition of, 66
  second derivative test for, 67
Minimum of a function:
  definition of, 66
  second derivative test for, 67
Moment of inertia:
  definition of, 106
  extended body, 107–110
  hollow cylinder, 117 (Exercise 3.21)
  homogeneous cylinder, 108–110
  infinitesimal, 107, 108
    integration of, 108–110
  of point mass, 106
  of several point masses, 106

Motion:
  with constant acceleration, 46, 62–66, 78–80
  of falling body, 46, 62–66
  of projectile in two dimensions, 70 (Exercise 2.25)
  simple harmonic, 47
  starting and finishing points, 102–103
  of vertically thrown projectile:
    downward, 80–81
    upward, 68–69

Nomenclature, derivative, 21–22
Notation:
  chain rule, 27, 29
  derivatives, 21–22, 40–41
  differentials, 47–48, 51
  exponential function, 76
  function at a point, 6–8
  functional, 4–5
  second derivative, 29–30, 45
  summation, 84–85

Operation:
  derivative, 23
  differential, 51

Parabola:
  downwardly concave, 68
  equation, 10
  graph, 9
Parameter, 16
Path of moving particle:
  circular, 16–17
    equations, 17
  coordinates as functions of time, 17
  as function of time, 15–17
  given by equation, 15–16

Path of moving particle (*Cont.*):
  projectile in two dimensions, 70 (Exercise 2.25)
Point:
  critical, 67
    derivatives at, 67
  rectangular coordinates of, 9
  starting and finishing, 102–103
  on x axis, 6
Position (*see* Path of moving particle)
Power of variable:
  derivative, 24–25
  differential, 51
  integral, 75
Product of functions:
  derivative, 25
  differential, 51
  and integration by parts, 76–77
Projectile:
  in two dimensions, 70 (Exercise 2.25)
  vertically thrown: downward, 80–81
    height as function of time, 69
    initial velocity, 68
    maximum height, 69
    time to reach maximum height, 69
    upward, 68–69
    vertical height, 69

Quotient of functions, derivative, 25

Radian:
  definition of, 12
  relation of, to degree, 13

Rate of change:
  average, 32–34
    connection of, with instantaneous rate of change, 35
    definition of, 32
    examples of, 32–34
    limit of, 34–35
  connection of, with derivative, 34–38
  connection of, with differentials, 50–51
  instantaneous: and acceleration, 45, 46
    connection of, with average rate of change, 35
    definition of, 34–35
    examples of, 35–38
    graph of, 37
    meaning of, 36–37
    at a point, 35
    with respect to time, 39–40
    summary of, 38
    and velocity, 40
  with respect to variable other than time, 43–44
  of work with respect to time, 54
Replacement of sum by integral, 96
Ring, circular, 55, 114

Second derivative, 29–31, 45–47
  notation, 29–30, 45
  operation of, 30–45
  with respect to time, 45
  summary, 47
  test for maxima and minima, 67
Shell:
  cylindrical, 108–109
  spherical, 56

Simple harmonic motion:
  acceleration, 47
  distance, 47
  velocity, 47
Sin x (*see* Sine function)
Sine function (sin x):
  cycle, 14
  derivative, 25
  differential, 51
  graph, 13–14
  integral, 75
  maxima and minima, 70
    (Exercise 2.24)
  period, 14
Slope:
  of curve, 59–60, 62
  of geometric tangent, 60–62
    related to derivative, 60–61
  of graph of distance as function
    of time, 63–64
  of graph of velocity as function
    of time, 65
  of straight line, 10–11, 59–60
Small angle approximation, 14–15
Specific heat:
  definition of, 104
  solid argon, 105–106
  temperature-dependent,
    104–105
Spherical shell, 56
Straight line:
  equation, 10
  graph, 11
    slope, 10–11, 59–60
    y intercept, 10
Sum:
  definite integral as limit of, 87,
    92
  of functions: derivative, 24
    differential, 51
    integral, 74
    notation, 85

Sum (*Cont.*):
  of infinitesimal elements, 94–96
  notation for, 84–85
  replaced by integral, 96
Summation notation, 84–85
Summation symbol, 84

Tan x (*see* Tangent function)
Tangent, geometric:
  angle made with x axis, 60–61
  connection of, with derivative,
    60–61
  at a point, 60–61
  slope of, 60–62
Tangent function (tan x),
    derivative, 25–26
Temperature:
  as function of time, 43
  gradient, 44
  increase in, 104–106
  infinitesimal interval of, 104
  initial and final, 104
  in rod, 43–44
  and specific heat, 104–105
Thermodynamics, first law of,
  52
Time:
  derivative with respect to,
    39
  function of, 38
  infinitesimal, 54
  meaning of, in physical
    problems, 38–39
  sinusoidal variation with, 47
  velocity as function of, 41–43,
    63–64, 79–80
Trajectory, 15
Trigonometric functions:
  definitions of, 119
  derivatives of, 25–26
    (Exercise 2.4)

Trigonometric functions (*Cont.*):
  differentials of, 51
  graphs of, 12-15
  identities of, 120-121
  inverse, 121
  sine, 13-14
    (*See also* Sine functions)

Variable:
  definition of, 1
  dependent, 2-3
  dummy, 89
  increment in, 19, 32-33
  independent, 2-3
    differential of, 48
  of integration, 74
    physical meanings, 103
  power of (*see* Power of variable)
Variables, independent, 5
Velocity:
  as function of time, 41-43
    63-64, 79-80
  graph as function of time,
    64-65, 82-83
  initial: and constant of
    integration, 80
    definition of, 68
  initial condition on, 80
  instantaneous: connection of,
    with derivative, 40, 42
    definition of, 40

Velocity, instantaneous (*Cont.*):
  derivative of, with respect
    to time, 45
  as rate of change of distance,
    40
  in simple harmonic motion,
    47
  summary, 42-43
  as slope of graph of distance
    as function of time, 63-64,
    82-83
  tangential, 16
  vertical, 69, 81
  of vertically thrown projectile,
    69, 81
Volume:
  of cylindrical shell, 108-109
  differential (*see* Differential
    volume)
  element of, 108
  of spherical shell, 56

Work:
  done by constant force, 53-54
    101
  done by variable force, 101-103
  element of, 54, 101-102
    integration of, 102-103
  infinitesimal amount of, 54
  rate of change with respect to
    time, 54